Advance praise for

She Rises Like the Sun
Invocations of the Goddess by
Contemporary American Women Poets

"*She Rises Like the Sun* beautifully communicates the power of the goddess to inspire rich, passionate woman-affirming poetry. The poems gathered here answer to our longing for images that name our deepest pains, most closely held secrets, most cherished joys. They acknowledge our moments of isolation, celebrate our experiences of communion. They are truly gifts of the goddess. The already loved favorites I had hoped would be included *are*, along with hitherto unfamiliar poems by which I have been moved—and taught."

> --Christine Downing
> Author of *The Goddess* and
> *Psyche's Sisters*

"Gratitude for poetry and the other ritual arts of spiritual practice, for these brave women artfully declaring the truth of their being, for Janine Canan's gathering of this collection."

> --Charlene Spretnak
> Author of *Lost Goddesses of Early
> Greece* and editor of *The Politics of
> Women's Spirituality*

She Rises Like the Sun

Invocations of the Goddess by Contemporary American Women Poets

EDITED BY JANINE CANAN

Foreword by Jean Shinoda Bolen, M.D. / Illustrated by Mayumi Oda

The Crossing Press
Freedom, California 95019

Library of Congress Cataloging-in-Publication Data

She rises like the sun. : invocations of the goddess by contemporary
  American women poets / edited by Janine Canan.
      p.   cm.
  ISBN 0-89594-353-0   — ISBN 0-89594-352-2 (pbk.)
  1. Goddesses—Poetry. 2. American poetry—20th century.
3. American poetry—Women authors. 4. Women—Poetry. I. Canan, Janine.
PS595.G54S48 1989
811'.54'080353—dc19   89-523
                                           CIP

CONTENTS

FOREWORD BY JEAN SHINODA BOLEN xv
ACKNOWLEDGMENTS xix
INTRODUCTION BY JANINE CANAN xxi

PAULA GUNN ALLEN
    Grandmother 1
    Creation Story 2
    Womanwork 3
    He Na Tye Woman 4
    The Blessing 6

MAYA ANGELOU
    Woman Me 7

BARBARA BROOKER
    Dear God 8

JANINE CANAN
    Inanna's Descent 10
    Creation 12
    Dear Body 13
    Our Lady 15

DIANE DI PRIMA
    Ave 18
    And Will You Hunt The Loba? 21
    Love Song Of The Loba 22
    Her Power Is To Open What Is Shut/Shut What Is Open 24
    The Poet Prays To The Loba 25
    Dream: The Loba Reveals Herself 25
    The Loba Addresses The Goddess/Or The Poet As Priestess
        Addresses the Loba-Goddess 27
    The Second Daughter: Li (Brightness) 27
    Loba As Kore In The Labyrinth Of Her Beauty/ The Loba
        Seeks The Mother In The Infinite Reaches Of Night 29

ELSA GIDLOW
    Let Wisdom Wear The Crown: Hymn For Gaia 31
    A Creed For Free Women 32

JUDY GRAHN
    Queen Of Wands 34

SUSAN GRIFFIN
    The Great Mother 41
    This Earth: What She Is To Me 44
    Our Mother 45

JOY HARJO
    Remember 47
    White Bear 48
    Grace 49
    The Book Of Myths 50

JANA HARRIS
    Beneath The Pole Of Proud Raven 52

ERICA HELM
    The Creation Songs Of Eurynome 55

LINDA HOGAN
    Desert 60
    Tiva's Tapestry: La Llorona 61
    Morning: The World In The Lake 62
    November 63
    First Light 65
    Scorpion 66
    It Must Be 68

CAROLYN KIZER
    Hera, Hung From The Sky 70
    Persephone Pauses 71
    Semele Recycled 73

MARY NORBERT KORTE

Rain To River To The Sea 77
This Room Of Trees & Moving Earth/ This Room Where
    No One Knows How Sky Begins 78
The Cat 80

MERIDEL LE SUEUR

Hush, My Little Grandmother 83
Behold This And Always Love 84
Rites Of Ancient Ripening 85
Let The Bird Of Earth, Fly! 88
Surround Of Rainbows 89
Make The Earth Bright, And Thanks 90

DENISE LEVERTOV

The Goddess 92
The Postcards: A Triptych 93
The Dragonfly-Mother 95

LYNN LONIDER

Invocation 98
Sistrum 99
Reading Of The Rattlesnake 100
Mediterranean Snake Admitter 101
The Swinging Goddess—Sally Ride; First American
    Woman Astronaut 103

AUDRE LORDE

The Winds Of Orisha 105
October 107
Call 108

MARY MACKEY

The Woman In The Moon 111
On The Dark Side Of The Moon 113
Betony 114
Cytherea 116

ROBIN MORGAN
The Two Gretels 120
A Ceremony 121
The Self (*from* The Network of the Imaginary Mother) 123

MARGE PIERCY
The Window Of The Woman Burning 130
Athena In The Front Lines 131
The Sabbath Of Mutual Respect 134
The Longest Night 136
O! 139
Let Us Gather At The River 140
I Saw Her Dancing 141
The Ram's Horn Sounding, Part 3 144

CAROL LEE SANCHEZ
Corn Children 146

MAY SARTON
The Invocation To Kali 149
Birthday On The Acropolis 154
The Return Of Aphrodite 157
When A Woman Feels Alone 158

NTOZAKE SHANGE
Sechita Had Heard These Things 159
I Sat Up One Night 160
Ancestral Messengers/ Composition 11 161

ALMA LUZ VILLANUEVA
Sisters 164
Creation 166
Winged Woman 168
Song Of The Self: The Grandmother 170
Sassy 171
The Object 172

The Politics Of Paradise 175
Splendid Moments 177
The Lake 178
The Crux 181

JULIA VINOGRAD
Motherdeath 183
Jerusalem 190
Reassurance 192
Anger 193
Celebration 194

DIANE WAKOSKI
The Ice Queen's Calla Lily Fingers 196
The Queen Of Night Walks Her Thin Dog 197

ANNE WALDMAN
Makeup On Empty Space 200
How I Became Biblical 204
Artemis 205

NELLIE WONG
Ode To Two Sisters In The Sun 206

ABOUT THE CONTRIBUTORS 209
BIBLIOGRAPHY 221

FOREWORD

Poetry evokes and expresses, nourishes and names what we intuitively know in the depths of the soul. In the metaphoric language of poetry, mythic images and evocative words come together to move us from one realm to another. Within the pages of *She Rises Like the Sun*, an anthology of contemporary American women poets, I found myself moved by poems to cross through the Mists to the realm of the Goddess, a place which lies within myself that is both deeply personal and archetypal.

In *The Mists of Avalon*, the novel by Marion Zimmer Bradley, Morgaine, the last priestess of the Goddess, could call the barge that would take passengers from the patriarchal world of Arthur and Camelot across the mists to Avalon and the realm of the goddess. At Glastonbury in England, the veil between the ordinary world and Avalon was for a time thinner, as this was the place where the barge could be called and one could make the crossing. Now that place of crossing lies within the psyche. The priestess is the woman poet whose words evoke the goddess, and the barge that takes us across to Avalon is the poem that moves us from our ordinary prosaic world into the timeless realm of the feminine.

Through these poems, perceptively chosen by Janine Canan who is herself a published poet and a practicing psychiatrist, we encounter the many aspects of the goddess: sacred, powerful, vulnerable, awe-ful, terrible, and most characteristically, embodied.

When She is addressed by name, that name evokes a particular image and form, which is one of the many faces and myriad expressions of the Goddess. Each poet-priestess invokes Her by a particular name; in this anthology of poems, She is called Gaia, Mother, Aido Hwedo (The Rainbow Serpent), Kali, Persephone, Tiva, Semele, la Llorona, Queen of Wands, Great Mother, Inanna, Ereshkigal, Lady of The Myriad Names, the Loba, Raven, Eurynome, Grandmother, the Woman, Iyetiko, He na tye, Lady, Lycia, Hera, White Buffalo Woman, God, She Rain, Dragonfly-Mother, Isis, Hecate, Mother Yemanja, Oshun, Oya, Orisha, the woman in the moon, Cytherea, Pallas Athene, Habondia, Artemis, Cybele, Demeter, Ishtar, Aphrodite, Au Set, Themis, Lilith, Thea, Bridgit, Cerridwen, Freya, Corn Maiden, Mawu, Amaterasu, Maires, Nut, Spider Woman, Shekinah, Winged Woman, the Creator, Motherdeath, Jerusalem, Ice Queen, Queen of Night.

In poem after poem there are moments of revelation, in which Goddess and woman partake of the same essence, when a woman finds the goddess in herself, when a knowingness, a gnosis, or intuitively felt wisdom about the nature of the Goddess or the connection that women have with the Goddess emerges out of personal experience, such as when earth or Nature and woman are as one; or when a woman herself becomes the Goddess as Maiden, Mother, Lover, or Destroyer. While poetry expresses meaning through analogy, poetry also expresses the literal numinous experience of the poet, for whom the Goddess was for a moment *really* present in nature, in herself, or in another woman.

Poetry with its rhythmic cadence and imagery has a power, similiar to drumming and music, to move us from ordinary reality and measureable time into that deeper place where we participate in time and have no sense of time passing. Like a familiar, forgotten fragrance, poetry tugs on us to remember something we once knew. May Sarton in "When a Woman Feels Alone," asks:

"What is the saving word from so deep in the past.
From as deep as the ancient root of the redwood.
From as deep as a woman's heart sprung open
Again through a hard birth or a hard death?

The words of a poem can be this saving word, providing us with an image, stirring up memory and yearnings, giving wisdom words to be known by. The poems in *She Rises Like the Sun* are invocations of the Goddess, which may stir dim memories of a time when for 25,000 years prior to the coming of the Indo-European peoples with their male warrior gods, the Goddess was worshipped and revered in Old Europe, and there were no gods; or they may invite us to recall pre-Judeo-Christian times, when both female and male deities were part of Greek and Roman Pantheons; or they may touch on a spiritual awareness held by Native Americans and other peoples who consider all life sacred, and the related-ness of all Life, something we also remember once knowing. As arche-types, goddesses are part of our human collective unconscious, and thus part of our own psyches—which is why the Goddess or goddesses are somehow familiar, and why the poet can evoke Her in us.

When I wrote *Goddesses in Everywoman* as a book about the psychol-ogy of women, I did not expect that it would also become a women's spirituality text. But because I used myths, metaphors, and symbols, which are the language of poet and priestess, it inadvertently illuminated a sacred and creative dimension in many women's psyches, as well as providing the psychological perspective it was meant to do. When sacred and creative centers in the psyche of women are stirred by the imagination, poetry, painting, sculpture, music, dance, and ritual naturally come forth. The Goddess is evoked, and She rises like the sun.

The subtitle of this book, "Invocations of the Goddess", reminds me of a ritual that has ended some of the women's retreats I have taken part in. This is a ritual in which we acknowledge the goddess in each other. The words are: "The Goddess in me beholds the Goddess in you. *Namaste*" (which means "I honor the divinity in you" in Sanskrit).

When I read the poems that moved me, there was a simultaneous, similiar recognition. I felt the Goddess in me as I met and beheld the Goddess in the poem and the poet. She Rises like the Sun.

Namaste,

Jean Shinoda Bolen

ACKNOWLEDGMENTS

I was walking through the labyrinthine display of appliqued goddesses, sculpted fetuses and painted cosmic creators at the perinatal psychology conference, when Someone grabbed me by the back of the neck and plunked me down with my poetry books on the floor, then propelled me through bookstores and libraries around the San Francisco Bay in search of poems invoking the Goddess. She hit like a thunderstorm and immediately arranged Herself into a symphony of women playing the music of the Goddess. Being with these women has been a deeply rewarding and joyous experience of beauty and community that has kept me going when many signs in the world around me might have filled me with dread. To all of them I am very grateful.

I also wish to thank my publishers Elaine and John Gill, who made this book possible; editor Yvonne Keller and writers Betty Roszak and Barbara Brooker for warm support and good suggestions. Special thanks to Diane Di Prima whose *Loba* poem provided the book's title; Patrice Wynne whose store *Gaia* was the scene of many key meditations; to Mayumi Oda for her wonderful artwork and Jean Bolen for her generous foreword.

But above all I wish to thank Margaret Clark, anthropologist, editor *extraordinaire* and beloved friend, who more than anyone has helped in the creation of *She Rises Like The Sun*.

INTRODUCTION

The image of the Goddess is everywhere in our culture today: in our art and literature, our mythology, our psychology, our history, our anthropology, our politics, our philosophy and, most significantly, our theology. Since the publication of Merlin Stone's *When God Was A Woman* in 1976, books published by feminist writers read like a crescendoing chant*:

Alone of All Her Sex
Ancient Mirrors of Womanhood
Bodhisattva of Compassion
The Changing of the Gods
Drawing Down the Moon
The Feminine Dimension of the Divine
Goddesses of Sun and Moon
Gyn/Ecology
Her Cycle of Transformations
Hygeia, Lost Goddesses of Early Greece
The Meaning of Aphrodite
The Sea Priestess, Seasons of Woman
The Spiral Dance, Woman and Nature
Womanspirit Rising!

(1978—1979)

Ariadne
Descent to the Goddess
Dreaming the Dark
Flight of the Seventh Moon
The Goddess, Goddesses,
The Goddesses and Gods of Old Europe
Goddesses in Everywoman
The Holy Book of Women's Mysteries
In Memory of Her
Inanna, Queen of Heaven and Earth
Medicine Woman, The Mists of Avalon

---

* Full references for the books cited below can be found in the bibliography.

The Moon and the Virgin
Mother Worship, Motherpeace,
The Politics of Women's Spirituality
Pure Lust, Sky Dancer, Sophia
Spiders and Spinsters
Woman as Divine, Woman: Earth and Spirit
The Woman's Encyclopedia of Myths and Secrets
Womanspirit!
(1980—1985)

Body Metaphors
The Book of the Goddess
Cakes for the Queen of Heaven
The Chalice and the Blade
Changing Woman and Her Sisters
The Crone, The Crone's Book of Words
Crystal Woman
The Cult of the Black Virgin
Dearest Goddess
Feminist Spirituality and the Feminine Divine
The Goddess Obscured
The Goddesses' Mirror
The Great Cosmic Mother
I Ching of the Goddess
Jaguar Woman, Jambalaya
The Kwan Yin Book of Changes
The Language of the Goddess
Laughter of Aphrodite
The Mother's Songs
The Mysteries of the Goddess
Pagan Meditations, Reinventing Eve
The Rose Cross and the Goddess
The Sacred Hoop
Star Woman
The Witches' Quabala
Woman Prayer—Woman Song, Womanguides
The Womanspirit Sourcebook
The Women's Spirituality Book!
(1985—1988)

There seems to be a great hunger in American culture for images of the Goddess, and a great generative force supplying them. When one beholds the books and statues and paintings evoking Her, one feels the enormous inner excitement they stir, and it seems we are all involved in some powerful collective event vaster than we can imagine. Slowly but irresistibly women are springing up, in covens or personal altars, reformed traditional churches, temples or ashrams, to proclaim a renewal of the queendom and the power and the glory of the Feminine. For it is to the "feminine" in us—the female and male heirs of that rich though denigrated legacy—that the values of life have been abandoned: Reverence for life-in-relation-to-death; awe toward the miracle of ever-unfolding creation—mineral, plant, animal and human; admiration for the vitality of nature and its counterpart in human creativity; devotion to relationships based on awareness of the interconnectedness of all life; commitment to the development of a human sensibility based on sensitivity, feeling, intuition and genuine thoughtfulness; joy in beauty, love and peace.

"Reverence for life", "human creativity", "the interconnectedness of all life", "sensitivity", "feeling", "intuition", "genuine thoughtfulness", "joy"—when have we ever heard a candidate for President of the United States utter these words? (When have we ever heard of a woman running for President?) And yet it is for precisely these words that we starve in this increasingly toxic culture of ours, which thrives like a cancer on "masculine" values of might, aggression, competition, mechanization, materialism and unfeeling reason. The peace-loving matrilineal American Hopi Indians have a word for the crisis in which we live: "Koyaanisqatsi". Its meaning, the Hopis continue to warn us, is that we live in a time dangerously out of balance, On the other side of the globe the goddess-worshipping Hindus call it the Kaliyuga, the Dark Age. And in the West, increasingly we are coming to know it as the long dark night of patriarchy.

In Riane Eisler's reconsideration of human history, *The Chalice and the Blade*, we read of the tens of millenia of peace, earth-rootedness, love of life, nature and beauty, among the egalitarian, agrarian, Goddess-worshipping, matricentric societies of Asia Minor, Thailand, Middle Europe and, later, Central America, that preceded the invasions of warring, hierarchical, slave-holding patriarchs who gradually conquered the world and maintain their powerful grip even today. Yet arching over many thousand years of patriarchal rule, we hear Her call once again. For we need Her. And indeed, from the deepest wells of our being She is gushing up in word and image to shift the balance, bringing light and harmony once more.

Of course, the poets and singers have always been Her priests. Was it not Hindu Sarasvati who invented the alphabet, and Celtic Brigit who presided over language? Did not Sumerian Nidaba invent the art of writing and the Greek Muses inspire all creativity? How then could we poets not be present at this long-awaited occasion? More than ever poets—even people who are not "poets"—are invoking Her name in poetry. The name by which She is invoked, the way in which She is spoken to varies endlessly. But She is being called. Among the poems in this collection, selected from the work of the strongest women poets writing in America today, we find songs that grieve for Her long absence, Her fall, the loss of Her memory; songs that describe an awakening, a vision, a sudden remembering, a personal call from Her. There are poems that invoke, beseech, praise and even reprimand Her as She returns and is encountered once again. There are poems spoken in prayer, whispered in intimate conversation and shouted in jubilation. And poems of personal transformation, of healing and rebirth that follow the discovery of the goddess within.

For a great social, psychological and spiritual rebirth of woman accompanies the return of the Goddess, as has recently been shown by Charlene Spretnak in her powerful collection of essays, *The Politics of Women's Spirituality*; by Jungian analyst Jean Bolen in her popular new psychology of women, *Goddesses in Everywoman*; as well as by Carol Christ in her incisive and moving work of theological critique and personal quest, *Laughter of Aphrodite*. But as far back as the eighteenth century, English physician William Alexander put it quite simply in his *History of Women*: "Whenever female deities have obtained a place in the religion of a people, it is a sign that women are of some importance; for we find in those modern nations where the women are held in the most despicable light that even their deities are all of the masculine gender."

Today the often quoted conclusion of Goethe's *Faust* takes on new and prophetic meaning: "The eternal feminine leads us on." After the Faustian debacle of World War Two, culminating in the American atomic bombing of Hiroshima and Nagasaki, Robert Graves published *The White Goddess*. In his concluding chapter, "Return of the Goddess", he asks the crucial question: "What, then, is to be the future of religion in the West?" He answers, "I foresee no change for the better until everything gets far worse. Only after a period of complete political and religious disorganization can the suppressed desire of the Western races, which is for some practical form of Goddess-worship, with her love not limited to maternal benevolence and her after-world not deprived of a sea, find satisfaction at last." But he warns, "the longer her hour is postponed, and therefore the more exhausted by man's irreligious improvidence the natural resources of the soil and sea become, the less merciful will her five-fold mask be, and the narrower the scope of action that she grants to whichever demi-god she chooses to take as her temporary consort in godhead." "Let us placate her in advance by assuming the cannibalistic worst," Graves concludes:

Under your Milky Way
    And slow-revolving Bear,
Frogs from the alder-thicket pray
In terror of the judgement day,
    Loud with repentance there.

The log they crowned as king
    Grew sodden, lurched and sank.
Dark waters bubbled from the spring,
An owl floats by on silent wing,
    They invoke you from each bank.

At dawn you shall appear,
    A gaunt, red-wattled crane,
 She whom they know too well for fear,
Lunging your beak down like a spear
    To fetch them home again.

It is perhaps not surprising that a man who expects the second coming of the Goddess would fear what form She might take after several thousand years of patriarchy. Indeed, in those rare poems by contemporary men in which She does appear, it is seldom without great ambivalence and fear on the part of the poet. I think here of two extremely powerful poems: Allen Ginsberg's "Stotras to Kali Destroyer of Illusion" and Robert Bly's "The Teeth Mother Naked at Last". Here are some passages from Bly's poem, written during the height of the Vietnamese War, but, alas, more appropriate than ever in this era of relentlessly mushrooming militarization:

It is a desire to eat death,
to gobble it down,
to rush on it like a cobra with mouth open.

It is a desire to take death inside,
to feel it burning inside, pushing out velvety hairs,
like a clothesbrush in the intestines—

That is the thrill that leads the President on to lie.

         *   *   *

These lies mean that something in the nation wants to die.
What is there now to hold us to earth? We long to go.
It is the longing for someone to come and take us by the
     hand to where they all are sleeping;
where the Egyptian pharaohs are asleep, and our own mothers,
and all those disappeared children, who went around
     with us on the rings at grade school.

         *   *   *

The mad beast covered with European hair rushes
     towards the mesa bushes in Mendocino County.
Pigs rush toward the cliff.
The waters underneath part: in one ocean luminous
     globes float up (in them hairy and ecstatic men);
in the other the Teeth Mother, naked at last.

In his excellent portrait of the patriarchal death-wish, with its passion-
ate exposé of American political corruption, violence to the earth and
moral depletion, is it not ironic that the poet calls that death worship by
the name of the Goddess? And where is Her creative aspect, the eternal
alternative to death? Cheerfully and more wisely, poet James Broughton
stands at the shore and calls out to Old Mother Sea, "Lady of Another
Think Coming":

I confess the wrongs of my head.
I repent its thoughtless notions.
Have you a tonic brain wash?
I am ready to mind my change.

Clearly the time for a change has come, and the time for the Goddess to speak. And it is in the women that She now speaks, in all of Her boundless variety. In this vibrant and beautiful collection of poetry dedicated to the Goddess, we find the enormous range of manifestation and sensibility through which She may be apprehended, as women explore the vast symbol of the goddess within, around and beyond us.

Opening the collection, poet Paula Gunn Allen, author of *The Sacred Hoop: Recovering the Feminine in American Indian Traditions*, invokes the goddess from the most ancient American creation stories:

> That dawn She came,
> riding the sun,
> humpback flute player heralding Her dawn
> the Corn, sweet maiden, riding
> the new day
> latest in a series
> of alternate paths....

And as She returns, "we return, immortal/ in our ancient disposition." "The water rises around us like the goddess coming home:"

> Storms of water, and we
> deluged
> singing
> hair plastered to our ecstatic skulls....

"How did I wait so long to drink," she asks.

Sublime poet Maya Angelou finds the goddess in her majestic vision of woman:

> Your smile, delicate
> rumor of peace.
> Deafening revolutions nestle in the
> cleavage of
> your breasts....

*   *   *

Your laughter, pealing tall
above the bells of ruined cathedrals.
Children reach between your teeth
for charts to live their lives.

In a fully fleshed-out version of this vision, a book-length poem entitled
Now Sheba Sings the Song, which unfortunately could not be included in
this anthology, Angelou invites us to enter and explore the vast and
luxurious landscape of Sheba:

From the column of my thighs
I take the strength to hold the world aloft....

       *   *   *

What I have not seen cannot be.
Sunsets and rainbows, green forest and restive blue seas, all
    naturally colored things are my siblings. We have played
    together on the floor of the world
Since the first stone looked up
At the stars.

       *   *   *

Oh my movement admits to
Lip smacking, finger snapping, toe tapping
Shoulder bouncing, hip throwing, breast thrusting, eye flashing,
Love of good and God and Life.

Barbara Brooker, author of *So Long, Princess*, addresses her own
personal god in the intimate prayer "Dear God":

Hello, God,
I think we've met
At several events....

And then, on that white rainy day
last year, remember?
We sat inside the yellow dream,

Thick wind winding your dress,
so violet, pretty
We talked....

Brooker's God is immediate, female and moral. She can talk to Her about her life and how to live. What about "hollow eyes,/ empty mouths,/ bone heads,/ stick fingers,/ rattle, rattle"? She is told to "comfort those festered limbs". Brooker knows how important it is to remind God of her existence, and to remind herself of God's: "I have your picture on my mirror. Your long/ silver hair is beautiful....I call you Lycia."

My own poems, selected from *Her Magnificent Body*, describe the descent of the Goddess, Queen of the Great Above, into the dark and mortal realm below, and Her eventual re-emergence. "Inanna's Descent", inspired by Sylvia Perera's *Descent to the Goddess*, retells the story of the patriarchal eclipse of the Great Sumerian Goddess, and at the same time tells the story of anyone's descent into a personal abyss. In "Creation" I am blessed with a dream-visit from the Goddess, "bringing silk sky, satin weaves, bright paintings, smooth scupture, stretching trees and the bountiful hills behind Her. Alongside me now She offers her magnificent body." In "Dear Body" the soul addresses the body with loving respect:

...And though you may never
fathom what I secretly am, may you—
who accepted the nature of existence itself—
stay with me in your lovely halo of death,
till I depart, dearest Body, my slave, my queen.

And in "Our Lady" I try to grasp the Goddess in all of Her incomprehensible being as creator and destroyer of the universe:

Guide me through chaos and though I cannot find you,
be with me as any creature in the field.

Now and always, living or dead,
on the vast arcs of energy certain and turbulent,
or lost tossed in your void, Great Wombed Mother,
for You will be whether I know it or not.

Diane di Prima's epic poem *Loba* has already become a classic of modern religious poetry. "A great geography of the female imagination," Adrienne Rich called it, based on the myth of the White Wolf:

> I turned to confront
> > to face
> > > Her:
> > > > ring of fur, setting off
> the purity of her head.
> She-who-was-to-have-devoured me
> stood, strong patient
> > > > recognizably
> goddess.
> > Protectress
> great mystic beast of European forest.

Chanting, the poet approaches:
> large gypsy mother, I lean my head on your back
> I am you
> and I must become you
> I have become you
> and I must become you
> I am always you
> I must become you

> > *ay-a*
> > *ay-a-ah*
> > *ay-a*
> > *ay-a ah ah*
> > *maya ma maya ma*
> > *om star mother ma om*
> > *maya ma ah.*

This extraordinary visionary work tells the powerful tale of the Goddess's return: "Now/ she rises, like the sun...." In "The Loba Seeks the Mother in the Infinite Reaches of Night", di Prima sings, "All things are possible within the mother:"

                splayed paths
                        spread like star's rays.
The Roads not taken.
                        Opening to us
as She opens
                        shd we dare.

Elsa Gidlow, "Poet Warrior" as she was called by her beloved mentor, Yeats' compatriot Ella Young, died recently, but she has left us her *Sapphic Songs, Eighteen to Eighty*, in which she wrote amply of woman's love of the feminine. "If this world," she wrote in her introduction, "with its exquisitely interacting life forms miraculously escapes the horror of nuclear insanity, I feel confident that women will more and more freely and joyfully express our erotic nature in its many facets from sensual to spiritual." Early on Elsa met her Goddess, "the Mother of all opposites", in nature, in dreams, in women and in herself. In her maturity she was to write, "Wonders and marvels come to pass/ When the Wise Woman wears the crown." And at the age of eighty-one, more powerfully than ever she invoked the divine in her "Creed for Free Women (And such men as feel happy with it)":

I, we, Mothers, Sisters, Lovers,
Infinitely small out of her vastness,
Yet our roots too may split rock
Rock of the rigid, the oppressive
In human affairs.

This is She
And being of Her
Thus am I.
Powered by Her,
As She gives, I may give,
Even of my blood and breath;
But none may require it;
And none may question me.

I am.
I am That I am.

Portraiturist of "The Common Woman Poems", poet Judy Grahn has more recently undertaken to create a new feminist cosmology. In *The Queen of Wands* (and its sequel *The Queen of Swords*), Grahn labors to reweave the threads of the old myths in order to recreate the mythic attitude. In the title poem we see a vision of creation as a vast magically interconnected web. The Queen of Wands is

a chalice of fire,
essential flame,
the Flama
and the stuff of which their new world will be made.

Sophia (Helen) they call me, enlightenment,
"God's light", wisdom, romance, beauty, being saved...

 *   *   *

And I am the Queen of Wands
who never went away
where would I go?

If anyone is the poet of the feminine—in all of its joy and its grief—it is Susan Griffin, author of *Like the Iris of an Eye, Woman and Nature: The Roaring Inside Her,* and *Unremembered Country*. The whole of her work, with its poignance and sensitivity, expresses the longing for Mother, for tenderness, and the perpetual, crushing encounters with the masculine. In this she is the spokeswoman of our times. At the pinnacle of her beautiful and moving prose poetry masterpiece, *Woman and Nature*, Griffin—who was surprised to find The Great Mother parachuting toward her in her first work—now immerses herself in the earth as a living sister, in an ecstatic union of mutuality:

As I go into her, she pierces my heart. As I penetrate further, she unveils me. When I have reached her center, I am weeping openly.... This earth is my sister; I love her daily grace, her silent daring, and how loved I am *how we admire this in each other, all that we have lost, all that we have suffered, all that we know: we are stunned by this beauty*, and I do not forget: what she is to me, what I am to her.

In a more recent poem from *Unremembered Country*, "Our Mother" is very present. She raises her large ear up to the sky and instructs us all to do this to avoid despair.

Joy Harjo, a poet whose muse is an ancient American spirit, reminds us to "Remember":

> Remember that you are this universe and that this
> universe is you.
> Remember that all is in motion, is growing, is you.

A woman whose life is ever in transit, flying in an airplane, she sees

> the white bear
> moving down from the north, motioning her paws
> like a long arctic night, that kind
> of circle and the whole world balanced in
> between carved of ebony and ice....

And though this momentary vision of wholeness cannot last, "Wind", she cries, "I am still crazy. I know there is something larger than the memory of a dispossessed people." And one day, on "the stolen island of Manhattan", "in these times when myths/ have taken to the streets," she finds the goddess:

> When the dawn light came on through the windows,
> I understood how my bones would one day
> stand up, brush off the lovely skin like a satin blouse
> and dance with foolish grace to heaven.

Jana Harris is a writer who specializes in the western American experience. Here she contributes a creation chant inspired by the Northwest Coast Indians. In "Beneath the Pole of Proud Raven" the Goddess creates herself, taking to herself glacier water, salmon skin, loon call, wolf claw, raven coat, woman fog, coal fire, whale bone, until She *is* glacier, fish, loon, wolf, night, fog, fire, mountain—*the power, the earth*—warning us to "beware", be *aware* of Her awesome power.

In a series of "Creation Songs", performance poet Erica Helm retells the lost myth of Eurynome, "Universal One", pre-Greek Creator of the Universe. First, Eurynome divides chaos into sky and sea; then, dancing on the sea, She makes her serpent consort Ophion out of wind; She gives birth to the egg of the universe, Ophion cracks it open, and the universe spills out. "It is good," says the Mother of all things, basking in the light of Her creation. From the mountain, Eurynome and Ophion savor the "fragrant earth below", adoring "the brilliant sky, sweet honey and riversong." But Ophion grows bored with beauty and harmony and claims ownership, then authorship. Impatiently Eurynome kicks him into the world pit, and creates this time a king *and* queen to rule in balanced harmony the planets of creation.

Linda Hogan, a Chickasaw Indian whose work is rich in native American spirituality, is developing a uniquely moving voice. Her earlier poems whisper as if the spirit of the earth itself, expressing a deeply authentic, exquisitely sensitive empathy with earth and life:

> That is what I teach my daughters,
> that we are women,
> a hundred miles of green
> wills itself out of our skin.

For she is like Tiva, whose fingers are

> ...flying away
> on the white hair growing
> on the awful tapestry of sky
> just one of the mothers
> among the downward circling stars.

Stronger, sharper, more recent poems speak with a new and confident, and sadder, power, as in "Scorpion" and "It Must Be". But Hogan never forgets to praise the fresh new morning, when she makes her offerings "to those who came before me,/ and to birds/ under the eaves,/ and budding plants":

> the grandmothers look out from those holes
> watching over us
> from there and from there.

In her well crafted portraits of herself as the Greek goddesses Hera the Wife, Persephone the Daughter, and Semele the Earth Mother, vital

Pulitzer Prize-winning poet Carolyn Kizer vividly conveys what it is like to be a goddess of the patriarchy. "I pitted my feminine weight/ Against God, his terrible throne," she cries in "Hera, Hung from the Sky". In "Persephone Pauses" (based on a later version of the same myth as "Inanna's Descent"), Persephone turns her back on her mother, Demeter, to make her yearly return to the dark underworld with her seducer, Hades. In "Semele" we find the earth goddess, shattered by the painful loss of Zeus' love, gradually re-assembling her parts until finally He calls her name, "like a thunderclap" their bodies meet, and making love they "are sweet and wholesome once more".

Mary Norbert Körte, formerly a Dominican nun, lives now in a northern California forest where she finds Isis, Demeter, Kali and Hecate. The Mother is in our songs, our cries, the drenching rain, the incandescent cat: "there are ways to see the startracks on every thing." Körte's finely crafted poetry is numinous with inner life. Like her cat, she

> speaks from a place
> of rumoured power a place
> just out the corner of watching
> and she guards her place her light....

Eighty-nine year old Meridel Le Sueur has lived through every year of the twentieth century. She is the author of numerous books, stories, articles and poems, and the great-grandmother of twenty-one. The abundance, beauty and strength of her life overflow in these poems selected from *Rites of Ancient Ripening* (1975).

> The white buffalo woman brings the
> sacred pipe of vision.
> Standing on the hill behold me
> Coming coming coming.
> Over the prairie breast I come
> sacred,
> Covered by a cloud of flowers.
> Behold what you see, my grandchildren
> Behold this
> And always love it.

Her great long poem, "Dòan Kêt", which means "Solidarity" in Vietnamese and was written during the Vietnamese War, is woman's reply to Bly's "Teeth Mother Naked at Last":

I saw the women of the earth rising on horizons of nitrogen.
I saw the women of the earth coming toward each other
                    with praise and heat
                              without reservations of space.
All shining and alight in solidarity.
Transforming the wound into bread and children.
In a new abundance, a global summer.

One of America's greatest living poets, Denise Levertov is renowned for the exquisite refinement of her music and moral vision. Punctuating the long arc of her creative *oeuvre*, which includes eighteen books of poetry, is the occasional, essential poem to The Goddess, "without whom nothing/ speaks in its own tongue, but returns/ lie for lie!" For Levertov's goddesses are her sources of truth, her true voices. Whether She is the Large Goddess who throws her across the room, the miniature statue on her desk who "stands between the worlds", or the Dragonfly-Mother "who darts unforeseeably/ into unsuspected dimensions", hovering in "a summer/ fertile, abundant, where dreams/ grow into acts and journeys", She's

a messenger,
if I don't trust her
I can't keep faith.

In her recently published *Clitoris Lost*, rebutting Milton's *Paradise Lost*, Lynn Lonidier explores the ancient terrain of the Cretan Snake Goddess and brings Her energy to bear in a series of crackling goddess chants and rituals, warning:

We won't pass
imagining its sound Wheels of
a lion-headed woman-driven
chariot drawn by lions
(revive) 'til once the
sistrum

```
sings
the
sistrum
sings.
```

"The Mediterranean Snake Admitter" tells how to create a sacred shrine for your long lost ancestor, the snake. "The Reading of the Rattlesnake" reports on the upsurgence of matriarchal behavior among children of the eighties:

```
         O it's
a dangerous world slowly
being infiltrated by diamonds,
curving rectangles on the
rattlesnake's back.
```

And her jazzy homage to "The Swinging Goddess" Sally Ride, first American woman astronaut, expresses her hope that as woman evolves, "centuries-slow Adam" will also learn to "birth compassion beyond what he's fucked lately, u-huh!"

Audre Lorde's invocations to the Goddess flare too with passionate anger. In an early poem she foretold the Goddess' return: "I expect some new religion/ to rise up like tear gas/ from the streets of New York..../ The high priests have been ready and waiting/ with their incense pans full of fire." Now in "The Winds of Orisha" she becomes one of Her high priests:

```
I will become myself
an incantation
dark raucous many-shaped characters
leaping back and forth across bland pages
and Mother Yemanja raises her breasts to begin my labor
near water
the beautiful Oshun and I lie down together
in the heat of her body truth my voice comes stronger....
```

In "October" she invokes Seboulisa, mother of power; and in "Call" she prays:

I have written your names on my cheekbone
dreamed your eyes   flesh my epiphany
most ancient goddesses   hear me
enter.

"I am a Black woman stripped down/ and praying/ my whole life has
been an altar," she cries in anguish that transforms into triumph: "Aido
Hwedo is coming."

On an entirely different wavelength, we hear the direct warm voice
of novelist Mary Mackey penetrating the old masculinist myths with
clear feminist perception that brims with the affection and mischievous-
ness, imagination and wit of a child. "I was the expanding universe", she
claims, "this is a true story/ I know/ I dreamed it". In "The Woman in the
Moon" her Grandmother advises, "tell all your daughters/ to build
something better/ burn kindling/ not carry/ keep one eye on the sky". And
her Demeter-like mother prophesies of her daughter: "she will cure all
wounds/ she will be Betony/ the spiked plant/ the wood mint/ the woman
alone/ who sanctifies." These mythic women are hopeful, helpful, happy.
But Cytherea, her sea goddess, "is not pleased/ she is not amused—
"about/ these/ bitter and dirty/ salty and dying/ these small mortal oceans/
it makes her weep to see them."

Feminist activist Robin Morgan, editor of two remarkable antholo-
gies, *Sisterhood Is Powerful* and *Sisterhood Is Global*, is also a brilliant
poet. Her poem "The Two Gretels" treats with humor the fear that women
feel on the adventure toward the "Great Good Mother Goddess". "A Cere-
mony" portrays two women wending their way through the wilderness to
create a ritual in a clearing of oaks in moonlight: "as if the moon and you
and I were slivers/ of one mirror, gazing on herself at last." And "The
Self", the concluding section of an intricate and masterly five-part poem
entitled "The Network of the Imaginary Mother", reveals an image of the
Self as all-powerful Spider Woman, who manifests as mother, daughter,
consort, child, spinner and creator of all: "There is nothing I have not
been,/ and I am come into my power./ There is nothing I cannot be."

In her collected poems, again and again Marge Piercy's strong
feminist voice evokes woman's spiritual power. "Woman", she cries,

you are not the bound witch
at the stake....

you are the demon of a fountain of energy
rushing up from the coal hard
memories in the ancient spine....

"Athena in the Front Lines" recalls the lost goddesses, Athena Promachos
whose helmet gleamed for a thousand years, melted down for coins;
Venus de Milo, reduced to advertisements. Woman, Piercy says, needs to
make her own art, to speak and hope her words will live. "The Sabbath of
Mutual Respect" pays homage to *all* of women's goddesses and possibili-
ties, Habondia, our true abundance, is freedom of choice. "The Longest
Night", affirming our darkest moments as the places where vision is born,
pays tribute to Hecate, goddess of the crossroads. And "O!" decribes the
birth of the goddess from the sea, "where love rules and women/ are free
to wax and wane and wander/ in the sweet strict seasons of our desires and
need." "Let Us Gather at the River" is the lament of the crone, the old
woman sitting by the river scolding corpses", who wishes one day to look
down and find the water beautiful, clean and clear again. "Oh, close your
eyes tight and push hard/ and evolve, altogether now," she encourages us
like a mid-wife, "We can/ do it if we try." And in one of her strongest and
most insistent poems yet, "I Saw Her Dancing", Piercy recalls a moment
in the sixties when she *saw* the Goddess Yemanja change herself into a
woman. Most recently—and much as Graves predicted, only more bene-
volently—She descends as a hawk, prying her silver beak into the poet's
heart, and it is the Shekinah. But finally Piercy says:

Like any poet I wrestle the holy name
and know there is no wording finally
can map, constrain or summon that fierce
voice whose long wind lifts my hair

chills my skin and fills my lungs
to bursting. I serve the word
I cannot name, who names me daily,
who speaks me out by whispers and shouts.

And we are grateful for the miraculous and sensible poetic grace that gives
her *all* of her names.

Poet and painter Carol Lee Sanchez, a member of Laguna Pueblo, attempts in her work to integrate native American intelligence into modern thought. Her poem "Corn Children" invokes the wisdom of the Corn Grandmothers, who warn against greed and ingratitude:

> you should never take more than you need.
> if you need some reeds for the new whisk broom
> then you go down to the river and tell the spirits
> all around you there, that you
> have come for some reeds.
> you must ask them for permission and
> then you must thank them for providing
> for you.

"We must respect everything put here. To restore harmony. To restore balance."

New Englander May Sarton is one of the most rational and traditional of the poets gathered here, and certainly one of the elders. In her prolific work that encompasses eighteen novels and seventeen volumes of poetry, we discover a well-developed relationship to the Goddess, who appears variously as Aphrodite, Athena, Kali and The Old Woman. Her "Invocation to Kali" deals with the most difficult spiritual problem, the existence of evil. "We have to reckon with Kali for better or worse," she says. Journeying to the kingdom of Kali, "the terrible place", the poet encounters her own violence and the violence of humanity. She prays:

> Kali, be with us.
> Violence, destruction, receive our homage.
> Help us to bring darkness into the light,
> To lift out the pain, the anger,
> Where it can be seen for what it is—
>
> The balance-wheel for our vulnerable, aching love.
> Put the wild hunger where it belongs,
> Within the act of creation,
> Crude power that forges a balance
> Between hate and love.

Help us to be the always hopeful
Gardeners of the spirit
Who know that without darkness
Nothing comes to birth
As without light
Nothing flowers.

Bear the roots in mind,
You, the dark one, Kali,
Awesome power.

In Ntozake Shange's exuberant feminist hit play *For Colored Girls who have Considered Suicide when the Rainbow is Enuf*, the Lady in Red cries, "i found god in myself/ & i loved her/ i loved her fiercely". Sechita, the barroom dancer, also experiences the ancient Egyptian goddess of love, creativity and harmony, coming to life in her as she dances in her red garters, black-diamond stockings, sequined taffeta skirt and graying slips, "catchin stars tween her toes". In the more recent "Conversations With The Ancestors", Shange's ancestors advise her to travel with the wind toward the sun: "we are sending sepia stallions/ headstrong appaloosas and cypress carriages/ to carry you home".

Alma Villanueva is a creation poet who worships the creative powers of woman and nature:

I celebrate the absence of mystery of
the 'eternal mystery of woman':
we are.

We are the trees of the earth
our roots stretching deep and strong,
the stone of the firmament,
sister to the stars
that gave birth to the soil.

In her stunning pregnancy poem, meditating on the slope of her bulging belly, she writes,

and I'm
bursting
to birth houses and trains and wheat and
    coal and stars
and daughters and trumpets and volcanoes
    and hawks and
sons and porpoises and roots and stone and
    worlds and galaxies
of humanity and life.

Since her early creation poems, Villanueva has written many beautiful goddess lyrics suffused with that rare and invaluable thing, *joie de vivre*. One enjoys her leisurely approach to her subject, the repose of her mind, her love of woman and pleasure. "Settle for nothing less," she advises, "than the object of your desire." "And when you hold the world in your hands, love Her." "She isn't pleased or displeased—She's been expecting you forever. She knows what you had to do to love your self."

First, I toast the sun, the full moon setting
in the west, the morning star melting
into violet, the sea at low tide,
exposing her slippery womb,

the scent of life, strong and stinging
like my own. Then, the Goddess
rises up from everywhere
and I toast her and laugh—.

Street poet Julia Vinograd has published numerous books of poems that—in the tradition of Emily Dickinson—compress the mind to consciousness, and these she sells on the streets for two dollars apiece (price has recently gone up). Limping down the street in her long black dress and cap, with her frightening aura and umbrella of light, she may be the dark evangelist of women's spirituality, a kind of utterly anomalous American Stevie Smith taken to the streets, or modernday Francoise Villon. A local institution as yet undiscovered by the nation, she is the archetypal Bohemian who finds the universe in the café, or on an abandoned street at night. It is therefore Julia who, even here, must bring the bad news:

Mother is dead.
Death is Mother.
Motherdeath comes to town.
Tell the world.
Tell all the worlds.
Pass it on.

In her astounding, award-winning, out-of-print *Book of Jerusalem*, on the other hand, she unveils the long lost feminine counterpart of the Hebrew God Jehovah, embodied as Jerusalem the Eternal City, beloved of the Lord and "compass of His shadow". A sort of incarnated Shekinah, Jerusalem is the beauty and unpredictability, joy and foreverness of life.

Diane Wakoski, author of too many books of poetry to count, is the unofficial poet laureate of Los Angeles, City of the Angels, the orange trees, the movie stars and the vast smog-filled suburban deserts. There, as a child, Diane met the Snow Queen:

not
as evil
but as refreshing goodness.
Her sky, a mirror of ice,
and its cracking splinters
NOT giving a false view of the world
but transforming
squalid or mundane reality into
an acceptable world.

The Ice Queen gave her hope, beauty and protection from pain. In "The Queen of Night Walks Her Thin Dog" the poet, with her marvelous imagination, is the Queen of Night, "running through the veil, /singing," with jewels in the back of her eyes.

Popular performance poet Anne Waldman, the "fast speaking woman", as she entitled one of her earlier books, brings her long-time experience of Tibetan Buddhism to bear in her throbbing incantation "Makeup on Empty Space":

I am putting makeup on empty space
pasting eyelashes on empty space

painting the eyebrows of empty space
piling creams on empty space

    *   *   *

I hang the black linen dress on my body
the hanging night, the drifting night, the moaning night
daughter of troubled sleep...
I hang up a mirror to catch stars, everything occurs to me
     out in the night in my skull of empty space

        *   *   *

there is talk of a feminine deity
I bind her with a briar
I bind with the tooth of a tiger
I bind with my quartz crystal
I magnetize the world.

Even emptiness is assuming a feminine face! Like a beautiful witch or
priestess or alchemist, magically the poet invokes Her. In "How I Became
Biblical" she calls the spirits of her ancient sisters, travelling "out of sound
to be one of milk and sorrow, and one of strength and metal". And in
"Artemis" she claims her goddess:

Chaste sprite, spicy nymph
wounding witch, any guise you wish
No hesitation, Dakini of Incantation
Command your spike deep in my heart

So I may ride, hunt, speak, shine
mid-wife your sting.

She Rises Like The Sun concludes with the solemn yet hopeful, gentle
questioning of San Francisco poet Nellie Wong's "Ode To Two Sisters In
The Sun," inspired by an old Chinese story about sisters who go to live in
a sun palace in the sky:

Two sisters, will you speak out?
Will you enlighten the universe,
saturate our tongues with song?

        *   *   *

Will I recognize you when we meet
and will our singing, our linking of hands
see me safely home?

Indeed, as long as the road home leads through fields of warheads,
radiation skies, poisoned soil, social oppression, and the ensnaring web of
science, materialism, mechanization and militarism, we have far to travel
to safety.

In this collection of poetry invoking the Goddess we see the power
that the image of the goddess increasingly holds for artists today, particu-
larly women artists. As individual as each poem is, the spirit of re-
emerging interest in the Goddess is apparent in all. And the Goddess of all
of these poems is vast, mysterious and inclusive, not small, dogmatic and
exclusive. These poems belong to men as much as to women, and tran-
scend that dichotomy in their reference to the forces that bind all life and
all beings. As Charlene Spretnak wrote in *The Politics of Women's
Spirituality:*

> The revival of the Goddess has resonated with so many
> people because She symbolizes *the way things really are*: All
> forms of being are One, continually renewed in cyclic rhythms
> of birth, maturation, death. That is the meaning of her triple
> aspect—the waxing, full, and waning moon; the maiden,
> mother, and wise crone. The Goddess honors *union and
> process* the cosmic dance, the eternally vibrating flux of
> matter/energy: She expresses the dynamic, rather than static,
> model of the universe. She is immanent in our lives and our
> world. She contains both female and male, in Her womb, as a
> male deity cannot; all beings *are part of Her*, not distant
> creations. She also symbolizes the power of the female body/
> mind. There is no "party line" of Goddess worship; rather,
> each person's process of perceiving and living Her truth is a
> movement in the larger dance—hence the phrase "The
> Goddess is All".

To explore with the poets of our time the symbol of the Goddess is a fascinating undertaking. We seem to find the poets turning Her around in their collective minds, viewing Her from all angles; viewing her from a great distance only to discover they are contained within Her. She is the earth, the grandmother, the mother, the daughter, the wife and beloved. She is the snake, the scorpion, the dragonfly, the cat and the wolf. She is the wise one, evolution, mystery, and the absence of mystery. She is the sky, the moon, the sun, and the rain. She is all of the arts. She is all colors and all races. She is the light and the dark. She is the dancer, the singer, the lover, the sufferer. She is life and She is death. She is goodness and evil; the void and creation. She is us. She is all.

In *She Rises Like The Sun* we see how true it is that art, as English philosopher Iris Murdoch has said, spontaneously manifests religion. Poetry, that quintessential literary art form, has always expressed humanity's current religious musings. The poems collected in this anthology constitute a new body of Western religious poetry. They announce the return of the Goddess, and contribute to the creation of a new religious myth that revives a vast network of old ones. In this new poetry women are experiencing the timeless Goddess in themselves and the world, and are addressing Her as a potent religious and moral force. The morality for which She stands and has always stood, is human gratitude for the inexpressibly great gift of life. She is love of life, love for the planet on which we live and love for all of the beings that live upon it. Without this love the human race will not survive. We all know this. Without taking care of the planet, Our Mother, we will not survive. As we create the Goddess within and around ourselves, we are committing ourselves to precious life.

Janine Canan

Hush, my little grandmother
I am a woman come to speak for you.
I am a woman speaking for us all
From the tongue of dust and fire
From the bowl of bitter smoke.
This is a song for strength and power.

Meridel Le Sueur
1900—

PAULA GUNN ALLEN

Grandmother

Out of her own body she pushed
silver thread, light, air
and carried it carefully on the dark, flying
where nothing moved.

Out of her body she extruded
shining wire, life, and wove the light
on the void.

From beyond time,
beyond oak trees and bright clear water flow,
she was given the work of weaving the strands
of her body, her pain, her vision
into creations, and the gift of having created,
to disappear.

After her,
The women and the men weave blankets into tales of life,
memories of light and ladders,
infinity-eyes, and rain.
After her I sit on my laddered rain-bearing rug
and mend the tear with string.

Creation Story

Light.
Stage of dawn.
Opening on new worlds
for the fifth time.
And not until they came forth
the Fourth Time was it ripe.
That dawn She came,
riding the sun,
humpback flute player heralding Her dawn
the Corn, sweet maiden, riding
the new day
latest in a series
of alternate paths
time of colors
rising.
And the sign of those days would be 4
She decreed, and the people arising
agreed. So we emerged into consciousness.
Born below in the place of nourishment
where those who have gone
wait, work, and come four days at a time
bringing the rain, coming home.
They fall on the gentle earth, sighing,
the squash, bean, corn sing of growing
and of grace. Pollen on the air golden
in that time, glowing, that return.
So on that day was given all this,
called Iyetiko, called Mother,
the clans, the people, the deer:
tracks left here and there
are signs.

Womanwork

some make potteries
some weave and spin
remember
the Woman/celebrate
webs and making
out of own flesh
earth
bowl and urn
to hold water
and ground corn
balanced on heads
and springs lifted
and rivers in our eyes
brown hands shaping
earth into earth
food for bodies
water for fields
they use
old pots
broken
fragments
castaway
bits
to make new
mixed with clay
it makes strong
bowls, jars
new
she
brought
light
we remember this
as we make
the water bowl
broken
marks the grandmother's grave
so she will shape water

for bowls
for food growing
for bodies
eating
at drink
thank her

He Na Tye Woman

Water.
Lakes and rivers.
Oceans and streams.
Springs, pools and gullies.
Arroyos, creeks, watersheds.
Pacific. Atlantic. Mediterranean.
Indian. Caribbean. China Sea.
(Lying. Dreaming on shallow shores.)
Arctic. Antarctic. Baltic.
Mississippi. Amazon. Columbia. Nile.
Thames. Sacramento. Snake. (undulant woman river.)
Seine. Rio Grande. Willamette. McKenzie. Ohio.
Hudson. Po. Rhine. Rhone.
Rain. After a lifetime of drought.
That finally cleanses the air.
The soot from our eyes.
The dingy windows of our western home.
The rooftops and branches. The wings of birds.
The new light on a slant. Pouring. Making everything new.

Water (woman) that is the essense of you.
He na tye (woman) that is recognition and remembering.
Gentle. Soft. Sure.
Long shadows of afternoon, growing as the light turns
west toward sleep. Turning with the sun.

(The rest of it is continents and millenia.
(How could I have waited so long for completion?)

The water rises around us like the goddess coming home.
(Arisen.) Same trip, all things considered, all times
and visions, all places and spaces taken into account
on that ancient journey, finally returned. The maps, the plans,
the timetables: the carefully guided tours into all manner
of futilities. Manners the last turn in the road: arid irony.

(Lady, why does your love so touch me?
(Lady, why do my hands have strength for you?
(Lady, how could I wander so long without you?

Water in Falls, misting and booming on the rocks below.
Tall pines in the mist, the deep carved caves.
Water in rivulets. Gathering speed, drops joining in headlong flight.
Unnamed rivers, flowing eternally underground, unchanging, unchanged.
Water thundering down long dry arroyos, the ancient causeways
of our faith. Drought over, at last. Carrying silt,
bits of broken glass, branches, pebbles, pieces of abandoned cars,
parts of lost houses and discarded dreams. Downstream.
Storms of water, and we
deluged
singing
hair plastered to our ecstatic skulls,
waving wild fists at the bolts hurled at us from above
teeth shimmering in the sheets of rain (the sheen)
eyes blinded with the torrents that fall fromthroughover them:
Rain. the Rain that makes us new.
That rain is you.
How did I wait so long to drink.

The Blessing

And so we meet again—
small ruffled birds
on the dying branches of the apricot tree
golden in metamorphosis:
honey in the air,
wine in the wind.
Between us, cold and light
agony and surprise—
deep places among the longago hills
things lost in labyrinthine memory,
not quite beyond recall though
perhaps beyond belief. Yet
we return, immortal
in our ancient disposition:
just this way Buffalo returns
to bless ancestral homes,
and long grass springs
again from Mother's breath,
waters again flow bright and clean.
The circles, however large their arcs,
close at last,
reminding us of what we've seen
and why we come round again.
And so memory, that
undying arabesque,
that blue and silver air of being
we helpless ride
forever circles the eternal pueblos
of our lives, restores the ruined
and faded kivas of our dreams.

MAYA ANGELOU

~~~~~~

Woman Me

Your smile, delicate
rumor of peace.
Deafening revolutions nestle in the
cleavage of
your breasts
Beggar-Kings and red-ringed Priests
seek glory at the meeting
of your thighs
A grasp of Lions, A lap of Lambs.

Your tears, jeweled
strewn a diadem
caused Pharaohs to ride
deep in the bosom of the
Nile. Southern spas lash fast
their doors upon the night when
winds of death blow down your name
A bride of hurricanes,
    A swarm of summer wind.

Your laughter, pealing tall
above the bells of ruined cathedrals.
Children reach between your teeth
for charts to live their lives.
A stomp of feet, A bevy of swift hands.

BARBARA BROOKER

Dear God

Hello God,
I think we've met
at several events.
I rsvpd,
I came the wrong day,
another wrong day.

And then, on that white rainy day last year, remember?
We sat inside the yellow dream, thick wind winding your dress,
so violet, pretty.
We talked, about a lot of things,
about the poor,
the sick,
AIDS,
the popemobile,
the withered eyes, tongues.

You said, climb their mountain,
hold their hand,
climb,
climb,
until you get to the top,
light a fire.

We lit a fire,
glowed out faces,
hollow eyes,
empty mouths,
bone heads,
stick fingers,
rattle, rattle.

While the wind blows,
warm the hill. Comfort
those festered limbs, treated
like old dogs, howling in the night, scraping
trees for food. I know. I saw.
They have courage, God. But you don't know courage
until you need it, you don't.

Anyways, God. I see another mountain. It's steep,
my breath is short. I haven't seen you lately,
I'll write you again. I'll rsvp, soon,
I will.
I have your picture on my mirror. Your long
silver hair is beautiful. Thank you for the
gardenia. I see your eyes behind the glasses,
I wear glasses too. We're about the same age
I think. I call you Lycia.

The sky is turning dark. Buildings poke the sun
turning dark.
Maybe a long rain,
I'll start climbing tomorrow. Oh, I see your shadow,
it's lithe, your hand is warm.

Climb, climb, climb. Air flowered, the sun so close.
Flower, flower, flower.

JANINE CANAN

~~~~~~

Inanna's Descent

Inanna, Queen of the Great Above, set her heart on Earth's deepest
ground. Turning her back on Heaven, She stepped down. "But your
safety?" anxious voices cried after her. "If I do not return, go to the
Fathers," She called back, already at the first gate. "On my way to the
funeral," She explained to the gatekeeper and the sandstone bars gave
way. Then down She went — through mud that tore the gold from her
ears. Down through granite arms that ripped the shirt from her breast.
Down through fire that singed the hair from her head. Down through iron
She thought was core that took her limbs. Farther and farther down She
hurled, through emptiness that drank her blood. Until at last She stood eye
to eye with Ereshkigal, Queen of the Great Below. That unpitying Eye
froze her heart and dazed She stepped through its pupil ringed with skulls
that chewed the flesh from her bones, as farther and farther She fell in the
hollow Abyss.

Far above, her consorts circled the houses of the Gods with drum and plea
and cry:
> *Heaven is hers!*
> *Earth is hers!*
> *She is a warrior,*
> *She is a falcon,*
> *She is a great white cow.*
> *She fought the dragon and slew it.*
> *She seduced the scorpion and tamed it.*
> *The golden lion slept at her side.*
> *She is the singer,*
> *She is desire.*
> *She is the mountain of silver, gold and lapis.*
> *On her hips tall trees grow, and grasses.*

From Her waters spout and savory grains.
Her lap is holy,
Her lips are honey,
Her hand is law.
Her breast pours heavenly rain.
She is the healer,
She is life-giver,
She is the terror, the anger, the hunger.
Fierce winds blow from her heart.
Hers is the thunder, the lighting, the glory.
She is the morning,
She is the evening,
She is the star.
She wears the gown of mystery.
Heaven is hers!
Earth is hers!
Who can argue?

No reply. The Gods were mute. Only one grumbled, "She who goes below must stay." The pines stiffened, as her corpse swung rotting on a pole. Ereshkigal threw back her leech-clawed head and roared with laughter. Her yellow lips foamed black then green, and her pupils grew enormous. Fastening on her the Eye of Guilt, She struck her thigh, howling: "Nothing! All is nothing!"

In his shrine at the bottom of the Sea lives wise and wily Enki. Nestled among clams and worms on black lava pillows that cover molten deeps, he dreams in the pale green glow. Hot and cold jets ruffle his skirts as he listens to the voices streaming through. That night he heard Ereshkigal's wanton roar drown Inanna's last cry. Aroused, he scraped fine silt from his fingernails and began to mould forms so small they passed through the narrowest crevasses of Earth's crackling crust. Entering Ereshkigal's Realm with plates of food and jugs of water, they heard her groan, "Oh my insides!" "Oh your insides!" they replied. "Oh my outsides!" She cried louder. "Oh your outsides!" they heartily returned. Ereshkigal grunted and groaned, writhed and retched—gruesome black lips contorted, eyes shining metal—as the tiny creatures echoed and re-echoed her grief, until slowly her great eyes softened and She was silent.

The gates opened. Inanna's dark corpse rose, swarming with demons. Over the sharp black hills the Evening Star stood watch. Clouds draped the desert. Ropy arms of cacti stretched toward the amber moon. Ducks flapped up over the inky waters. Passing over the broad and sleeping plain, She rose through mists over flooded fields of apples, dates, figs and grapes, and over the stocky houses. Rising higher, She saw the rivers turn milky, the bushes glow, the mountains crowned in pink, Earth a resplendent jewel green. In the clear night sky Inanna awaited the coming of morning light.

Creation

Twelve years old, I lie in my bed. How far does the sky go, the dark, stars arcing over my head? Something moves forward I can't take back to Mother or Father, and what I carry on will not return to me. Stars appear through the ceiling. Shadows move restlessly, avocado's large hands reach through the window, the house echoes inside me. Mother roams darkly from floor to floor. Father passes through, opening windows—he wants to throw out the old things, the unused. I fear for my doll, the quilt that Grandmother made, the handrolled pillow embroidered with blue. I tell him, "No". I leave home.

★

Now I must search the stars alone. I am no astronomer. From my bed I imagine great spaces: fiery Sun, moon-circled Earth, gassy Jupiter with frozen crust, myriad-silver-ringed Saturn. A galaxy of suns moves milkily downstream— dusty white snake coiling in dark, emblem that bejewels a giant slowly stepping through space. I see the wall that surrounds us with the end: Earth can't last, the Sun will die, other suns cool and go. At the edge of my bed I look down—it goes all the way. I see the poets there, lovers weeping in the wind. I hear a voice: 'You're made of nothing. You're the nothing made, nothing made you."

★

I have fallen asleep. A large Woman beckons. "Warm enough?" She asks, motioning me closer. She leans over laughing. She knows what I am thinking.

But She moves on through like the waves—bringing silk sky, satin weaves, bright paintings, smooth sculptures, stretching trees and the bountiful hills behind her. Alongside me now, She offers her magnificent body. I lay my weary head on her breast and touch the beautiful curving mouth, the fine hand and generous thigh, entering the pool of her pleasure. "Are you going away?" I ask. "What do you mean?" "I want you *here*," I reply. "Then *say it!*" She commands. And I wake in my room, streaming with sunlight.

Dear Body

Dear Body, gazing in the mirror it is you
that I behold with thankfulness.
You have been faithful these forty years.
With only a sore knee at puberty, some intestinal
rumblings before authority and teary outpourings
in the face of love, have you occasionally
asserted independence, disapproval, disregard of me.

Nor can I seriously object to the lines in your brow
that reveal where I have been thinking,
or to the downward curve of your mouth
that indicates grief I have carried since birth.
Your nose I thought too wide, has lengthened with time
that forces decision, and your white thighs
that frightened me, console me through darkening nights.

What good shoulders you have, I admit;
your soft breasts amaze me, and curving mortal hips.
When I see you naked so, still scarcely known,
I wonder, have I not served you well enough,
neglecting, depriving you of proper lovers—
surging, languorous caress of the bluegreen ocean,
the wild and powerfully exacting dance.

What a different story had I lived for you,
my devoted, solid, healthy Body,
with your hands of a potter or a surgeon,
strong enough to gather grain for a life of simple
satisfying eating. What patience you have shown
this lethargic, sedentary, moody being
who borrowed you, she claims, for higher reason.

Sitting waiting, while she thinks and dreams,
craving only quiet spaces, beauty in which
to lose herself on ever longer, more voluptuous
and deeper journeys, you must be a saint.
With your delicate, hyper-sensitive nerves—
painstakingly cultivated by erratic Mother Karma
who one moment forgets, the next grips violently,

so aware everything irritates or gives you
overwhelming pleasure, ecstatic wicked Body,
maniacally driven from one unreachable extreme
to another, isn't it obvious how, torn
between joy and terror, you became a poet,
passionately vibrating instrument, house
of the certain yet doubting, ever shifting eye.

Earthbody, brief spouse, what a strangely
inconvenient marriage. Yet you are my only
true support. And though you may never
fathom what I secretly am, may you—
who accepted the nature of existence itself—
stay with me in your lovely halo of death
till I depart, dearest Body, my slave, my queen.

Our Lady

Lady, how can I speak, my mouth silent
as the hills, dumb with fear and desire?
Lady of the Myriad Names, your beauty and destruction
freeze my heart. How can I approach You

from the city paved with bone? Highways roar
with trucks of nerve gas, rivers carry poisoned fish
and human heads—villages wrecked, people starving,
war missiles planted throughout the earth.

Shall I call You Dachau? Our Lady of Hiroshima?
For the skies are fumed with flesh,
Horrible Kali, Wretched Ereshkigal, Suffering One!
You wove the world of dark and light,

made the ways illumined and unknowable,
No Lady—of appetite, of difference, of need.
When You move the volcano rumbles, hurricanes blow,
clouds burst, rain falls, rivers rush and earth shudders,

Lady of All That Is. Bringing life to emptiness,
You cooled the fiery earth—who boldly made
orange sky, the blinding light—and made
the rocks where trees and grasses, poppies, broom

and waving mustard grow; candelabras of magnolia,
lavender cones of lilac, coral camelias, cascades
of acacia, purple crocus, yellow daffodil, pale cherry
and lacy alyssum. Into air you sent shimmering-winged

dragonfly, darting hummingbird, crying quail,
great eagle, blue heron and the red-tailed hawk
ever circling. Magnificent Lady, your mouth is trembling,
aging, more vulnerable than before. Behold:

Swift scorpions, sweet lobsters, thinking octopi,
shy whales and schools of diving dolphin;
solitary deer sauntering round radiation lab in moonlight,
wing-eared elephant, prowling lion and waiting dog.

You made them, Lady of Visions, who now destroy.
Strange machines exit your mighty thighs
and all of earth is afraid. Through the atmosphere's
decay, brass sunlight bathes harshly.

And through time the poets cry: Sappho, Tu Fu,
Kabir, Hölderlin. Do You hear Emily
whose heart pours such longing—in the night she saw
your body naked and your arms were rivers of light!

Smiling Lady, Aphrodite, whose face is turned away,
forbidden now. Like her, I have been wandering
in your marshes, like the insect, stumbling lover
in the wet dark flower. —So take me,

Unattainable and Only Lady, over your great loom
and weave me according to design. Guide me
through chaos, and though I cannot find You,
be with me, as any creature in the field,

now and always, living or dead,
on the vast arcs of energy certain and turbulent,
or lost tossed in your void, Great Wombed Mother,
for You will be whether I know it or not.

Bring love, fertility and warmth to my frozen soul
and fill heart's empty bed, though a small thing
in the enormity of your unfolding desire,
Lady of the Universe, Kind Lady, Kwan Yin,

Mother of God, of all the gods, avatars, saints,
the childish artists who crave to touch your shape,
even of the evil ones, crushed in your inscrutable heart.
Wise Sophia—Shekinah—hear my prayer

and when I drop my body into yours,
snuffed in the scents of your magnificent dream—
as loss upon loss gushes up from your unfathomable depths—
clasp me in your infinite gaze, Lady of All Knowledge.

DIANE DI PRIMA

Ave

O lost moon sisters
crescent in hair, sea underfoot do you wander
in blue veil, in green leaf, in tattered shawl do you wander
with goldleaf skin, with flaming hair do you wander
on Avenue A, on Bleecker Street do you wander
on Rampart Street, on Fillmore Street do you wander
with flower wreath, with jeweled breath do you wander

        footprints
                shining mother of pearl
                                behind you
moonstone eyes
            in which the crescent moon

with gloves, with hat, in rags, in fur, in beads
under the waning moon, hair streaming in black rain
wailing with stray dogs, hissing in doorways
shadows you are, that fall on the crossroads, highways

jaywalking do you wander
spitting do you wander
mumbling and crying do you wander
aged and talking to yourselves
with roving eyes do you wander

hot for quick love do you wander
weeping your dead

      naked you walk
      swathed in long robes you walk
      swaddled in death shroud you walk
      backwards you walk

        hungry
        hungry
        hungry

      shrieking I hear you
      singing I hear you
      cursing I hear you
      praying I hear you

you lie with the unicorn
you lie with the cobra
you lie in the dry grass
you lie with the yeti
you flick long cocks of satyrs with your tongue

    you are armed
    you drive chariots
    you tower above me
    you are small
    you cower on hillsides
    out of the winds

pregnant you wander
barefoot you wander
battered by drunk men you wander

    you kill on steel tables
    you birth in black beds
        fetus you tore out stiffens in snow
        it rises like new moon
        you moan in your sleep

digging for yams you wander
looking for dope you wander
playing with birds you wander
chipping at stone you wander

I walk the long night seeking you
I climb the sea crest seeking you
I lie on the prairie, batter at stone gates
calling your names

you are coral
you are lapis and turquoise
your brain curls like shell
you dance on hills

    hard-substance-woman you whirl
    you dance on subways
    you sprawl in tenements
    children lick at your tits

you are the hills, the shape and color of mesa
you are the tent, the lodge of skins, the hogan
the buffalo robes, the quilt, the knitted afghan
you are the cauldron and the evening star
you rise over the sea, you ride the dark
I move within you, light the evening fire
I dip my hand in you and eat your flesh
you are my mirror image and my sister
you disappear like smoke on misty hills
you lead me thru dream forest on horseback
large gypsy mother, I lean my head on your back

    I am you
    and I must become you
    I have been you
    and I must become you
    I am always you
    I must become you

ay-a
ay-a ah
ay-a
ay-a ah ah
maya ma maya ma
om star mother ma om
maya ma ah

And Will You Hunt the Loba?

And will you hunt the Loba?
Fools, will you use
lance, spear or arrow, gun or
boomerang? Think you she can be caught
in nets of love? She rides
the crescent moon like a flat-bottomed boat
in the stormy well of the sky
Will you fish for her? Do you hope
to wrap you warm in her pelt
for the coming winter?

Do you dream
to chew shreds of her flesh from inside of her skin
turn inside out her gut, suck juice
from her large, dark liver? Will you make a cap
of her stomach, necklace of her spine?

Look, she lies on her back in the sand like a human woman
the huge saguaro cactus bends to her, her love cry
darkens the mesa. Desert air grows black. Now
she rises, like the sun, she flicks
her tail, he is her black raincloud, he is
Señor Peyotl, grinning. Hand-in-hand
they run over the glassy yellow edge
of your horizon. . . .

After her! Whales-tooth & abalone
jingle as you give chase, yr horse
turns to tumbleweed, the mountains
smell of her breath, once again it is written
NOLI ME TANGERE in jewels
across the sky.

Love Song of the Loba

O my lord, blue beast
on the pale green snows, see
I have been running to keep up
w / you
        I have been
                running to find you
my tongue
        scours ice your
                tracks made
I drink
    hollows of yr steps,
                I thought
many a dark beast was you only to find
perfume of your fur, bright cloud
of yr breath not there, they are
flesh & clay, heavy dross, they do not
fly
    in the wind,
             see I have flown
to you, do you
        lurk in night
                do you sail
to sea on an ice floe
            howling sacred songs

O my lord, my good
                    dark beast
                                        how is it
I cannot taste you
                    wraith & shadow
tripleheaded
                    blind god of my
                                        spirit, you burn
blue flame on the
                    green ice, long shadows
lick at yr eyes
                    yr fur like arctic night
                                        the fire
of your song

I will circle the earth,
                    I will circle the
                                        wheeling stars
keening, my blue gems
                    shoot signals
                                        to yr heart:
I am yr loved one, lost from eternity
                                        I am
yr *śakti*
            wheeling thru
                        black space
I, the white wolf,
            Loba,
                        call to you
blue mate,
            O lost lord
                    of the failing hills

Her Power Is To Open What Is Shut
Shut What Is Open

Her power is to fall like razors
on the fine wind of yr spirit
Still water
        in the current,
                unmoving air
that the wind blows thru;
hers is the fire that clings, but does not
consume, dark fire that does not
light the night.

Torches in her labyrinth
                throw shadows
on ice-cut walls. Flickering stalactites
cut out of garnet.
          Her bower
lurks in the unseen muddy places
of yr soul, she waits you under the steps
of yr tenement.

         She gleams
in the wildwood where you have not dared
to walk. Wild yew & blackberries
tight, dried meat
of skinny winter deer, these
she holds out, like a key.
           Her door
cannot be found, it is close-shut, it crumbles
it wafts in wind. Her power is to raise
the pale green grass of spring, the pale wildflower
carpets which fly starward like primroses w / dogs
asleep on them. Her power is in spittle
& in the lentil,
          it rises like smoke
from the reopened furrow. She terraces the hills
w/ her glance, her white breast gleams
in mossy caves you remember where the smoke
curled on the greenwood fires

The Poet Prays to the Loba

O Lady
the hem of whose garment
is the sky, whose grace
falls from her glance, who gives
life from the touch of one finger
O Lady
whose hair is the willow, whose breath
is the riversong, who lopes
thru the milky way, baying, stars
going out, O
Lady whose deathshead holds a thousand eyes
eye sockets black imploded stars, who trails
frail as a northern virgin on the mist, O
Lady fling your bright drops to us, emblems
of your love, throw
your green scarf on the battered earth once more
O smile, disrobe for us, unveil
your eyes

Dream: The Loba Reveals Herself

she came
to hunt me down; carried down-ladder trussed
like game herself. And then set free
the hunted turning hunter. She came

thru stone labyrinths, worn by her steps, came
to the awesome thunder & drum of her
Name, the LOBA MANTRA, echoing
thru the flat, flagstone walls
>   *the footprints*
>   *footsteps of the Loba*
>   *the Loba*

drumming. She came to hunt, but I did not
stay to be hunted. Instead
wd be gone again.   silent
children in tow.

she came, she followed, she did not
pursue.
        But walked, patient behind me like some
big, rangy dog. She came to hunt, she strode
        over that worn stone floor
tailgating, only a step or two
                        behind me.

I turned to confront
        to face
                Her:
                        ring of fur, setting off
the purity of her head.
she-who-was-to-have-devoured me
stood, strong patient
                        recognizably
goddess.
        Protectress
great mystic beast of European forest.
green warrior woman, towering.
                        kind watchdog I cd
leave the children with.
                Mother &sister.
                Myself.

The Loba Addresses the Goddess / or
The Poet as Priestess Addresses the Loba-Goddess

Is it not in yr service that I wear myself out
running ragged among these hills, driving children
to forgotten movies? In yr service
broom & pen. The monstrous feasts
we serve the others on the outer porch
(within the house there is only rice & salt)
And we wear exhaustion like a painted robe
I & my sisters
                    wresting the goods from the niggardly
                        dying fathers
healing each other w / water & bitter herbs

that when we stand naked in the circle of lamps
(beside the small water, in the inner grove)
we show
no blemish, but also no superfluous beauty.
It has burned off in watches of the night.
O Nut. O mantle of stars, we catch at you
        lean   mournful
        ragged   triumphant
            shaggy as grass
our skins ache of emergence / dark o' the moon

The Second Daughter: Li (Brightness)

You enter power, but I am here before you
standing in what's left of grace on this planet
thc bits shored up, to form a circle of light
I cannot abdicate, even for you
                    come, join us!

You enter womanhood, I am a woman
to greet you, invest you, praise you
(there are oils for your skin, your hair)
I have not grown old suddenly before your eyes
          have not the courtesy to be decrepit
                    small
          in the wind at my back & yours
I have dances still to dance—do you dance?
          how the lights
          dance in you, eyes & skin
                         & brights of your hair
How your anger dances!

See how my skin
          like yours
                    takes on its sheen
after lovemaking
                    see how we glow!

The circle which is a spiral
stretches out
                    to the star of Isis
it is the stair of Light
                    in the upper parts glow
the Grandmothers
                    laughing
The Ancestress reaches her hand
to draw us up.
                    She is white vulture
                         with spiral neck

          These years are the windings
of Light
          our flesh flickers & changes
like flame.
          Like flame, it holds us fast.

The myth of mother and daughter is not a myth of overthrowing
(as in myths of the son & the father). . . but one of loss & recovery.
For there are realms & realms, in which the daughter rises to
self-knowing, to equal status with the mother — & in the feminine
universe, while some of the realms may be distant — "removed" —
none is out of bounds.

Loba as Kore in the Labyrinth of Her Beauty
The Loba Seeks the Mother, in the Infinite
Reaches of Night

This is a journey to Egypt
Secret, prolonged, & varied as the paths
of planets out of orbit, brushed aside
                    by demon Chance
This is internal labyrinth of Nuit
                    her bowels
thru which stars fall to birth.

For all fall is the fall
                    out of bright twilight of her womb
to the dark & light
                    below

All things are possible within the mother
We differentiate
                    we lose the Chance
her demon son: splayed paths
                    spread like star's rays.
The Roads not taken.
                    Opening to us
as She opens
                    shd we dare

This Road to blackest memory
     the fountain
whence Egypt sprang
       & powers of Sirius
Dog Star days that fell once on the earth
This is a journey backwards to beginning
Milke of the stars
      first tentative slow days
when Nuit was virgin
     & only Woman
         cd win her

the wolf Anubis
      Opener of the Ways
         She-wolf that climbed familiar
to that lap
    turning the faceted jewel
         then light
           now time
Splayed, raying, spinning path of Light
       now frozen
Pathways of Time
     on which we labor.
      Finite.

ELSA GIDLOW

Let Wisdom Wear the Crown: Hymn for Gaia

When the Wise Woman wears the crown
Marvels innumerable come to pass:
The sun rises in the East;
Seeds, well sown, swell,
Bring forth grass,
Oaks, lilies.

                  Earth's children moan
In grief; laugh when they are glad.
Wonders and marvels come to pass
When the Wise Woman wears the crown.

Water flows down hill,
Finds its level on the plain
When the Wise Woman is queen.
Tigers and wolves kill
And none is moved to complain
If mild nourish fierce.
                  As frost is chill

And fire burns, babes grow into women,
Sage and Child laugh, fear no bane
And find no thing to be ill.

The heart, untaught, moves the blood;
Sap of love quickens male flower
To seek female rose, rose to receive.
Unguided, the new-born knows its food.

The eye sees. Brain feels its particular power
As bare stalk knows when to bud
And death to come in its time.
Marvels, marvels, miraculous dower
And plenitude of incalculable good—

We know these to be ours,
We sing, dance on the green,
When Wisdom wears the crown,
When the Wise Woman is queen.

A Creed For Free Women*

I am.
I am from and of The Mother.
I am as I am.
Wilfully harming none, none may question me.

As no free-growing tree serves another or requires to be served.
As no lion or lamb or mouse is bound or binds,
No plant or blade of grass nor ocean fish,
So I am not here to serve or be served.

I am Child of every Mother,
Mother of each daughter,
Sister of every woman,
And lover of whom I choose or chooses me.

Together or alone we dance Her Dance,
We do the work of The Mother,

She we have called Goddess for human comprehension.
She, the Source, never-to-be-grasped Mystery,
Terrible Cauldron, Womb,
Spinning out of her the unimaginably small
And the immeasurably vast —
Galaxies, worlds, flaming suns —
And our Earth, fertile with her beneficence,
Here, offering tenderest flowers.
(Yet flowers whose roots may split rock.)

I, we, Mothers, Sisters, Lovers,
Infinitely small out of her vastness,
Yet our roots too may split rock,
Rock of the rigid, the oppressive
In human affairs.

Thus is She
And being of Her
Thus am I.
Powered by Her,
As she gives, I may give,
Even of my blood and breath:
But none may require it;
And none may question me.

I am.
I am That I am.

*And such men as feel happy with it.

JUDY GRAHN

The Queen of Wands

And I am the Queen of Wands.
Okay.
Here is how the world works:

It is all like nets.
Ever golden, evergreen
the fruits fall
into hands-like-nets
the fish are hauled
into jaws-like-nets
the insects crawl
into claws-like-nets

and the thoughts fall
into minds-like-nets
it is all like nets.

On the other hand
a spider lives in the topmost branches of a pine,
her house a god's eye gleaming among the needles.
On hot days
she pays out her line and
twirls on down
to the surface of the lake or pond

to get a little drink of water
and to wash her face. She's such an
ordinary person.

The trees line the earth, great and small,
dogwood, plane, maple, rubber,
the elegant palm. The scrubby oak. The elm.
We're ordinary persons, too. We have our
long time friends across the distances,
our urgent messages and our differences.

And we have our parties.
We sugar up our petals just to get the probes of bees in us.
Most green ladies love everything the whipping wind can give them.
The avocado tree hung with her long green breasts,
she aches for fingers pulling at her;
the cherry, peach and nut trees bent with swollen balls
long for hands and mouths and claws;
the fig tree with her black jewels tucked between her
hand-shaped emerald leaves, is happily
fondled by the dancing birds, wild and raucous and drunk on
natural fig wine.

Almost any summer morning
sun beams fall into my arms like lovers
giving me everything they've got
and they're so hot, oh honey
I take it all

give it to me, baby
is my song.

And I am the Queen of Wands.
The people honor me.
I am the torch they hold over their own heads
as they march march like insects
by the billions
into the bloody modern world,
over discarded corpses of their ages past,

always holding me, aloft or in their arms,
a flame in the hand of the statue,
a bundle of coals
in their inflammatory doctrines, calling me
a chalice of fire,
essential light,
the Flama
and the stuff of which their new world will be made.

Sophia (Helen) they call me, enlightenment,
"God's light," wisdom, romance, beauty, being saved,
"Freedom" and the age of reason.
Progress, they call me, industrial revolution,
"People's rule," the future, the age of
electronics, of Aquarius, of the common man and woman,
evolution,
solar energy and self-reliance. Sexual self-expression.
Atomic fission, they call me, physics, relativity,
the laser computations in an endless sky of mind,
"science," they call me and also emotion, the aura of
telepathy and social responsibility, they call me
consciousness, "health," and love
they call me, bloom of Helen.
Blush upon her face, and grace.

And here I am a simple golden shower.
And here I am only a spider
webbing their minds
with pictures, words, impulses,
feelings translated into moral imperatives
and rules for living, like leaves
upon a tree, spread to catch the sun's attention.

They (the billions of people)
dance like Fairies on my smallest
twiggiest branches
whistling in each other's ears,
collecting and dispersing
seeds, wearing gold and

pretty clothing, worrying and not
really noticing all the other worlds
around them
how the sun center of my eye sews them,
how the silver dream filaments direct them,
how their own thoughts connect them, how
the baton smacks their knees to make them
move their feet, that baton
at the end of the claw
of the Queen of Wands.

And I am the tree
with candles
in its fingers
the tree with lights
Menorah
Yule-flame
tree of life

the tree-shaped
candle-holder
on the mantle
on the altar
on the flag of being.

And I am the Queen of Wands
who never went away
where would I go?

the flame is central
to any civilization
any household

any bag of bones. Any motley mote
you've got, of
little mustard seed can grow
into a yellow spicy flame
as you must know.

The sun is a weaver
and the rock earth her instrument.
Slender-fingered threads of light
and heat, dance like birds
shuttling.
Winds and the rain,
seeds and feet and feathers
knit the knot
making the great coat,
the coat of all colors.

The coat of all colors;
over the whole earth, a caught fire
of living logs, brown and red,
tan and white, black and yellow
bobbing like a forest;
each a magic stick with
green flame at its tip

a green web
my leaves, my green filaments
like fingers spread
to catch the sun's attention, spread
to catch the sun like thread,
like sexual feelings, like
the gleam from an eye, or an idea.

And I am the Queen of Wands
I am who stands
who always will
and I am who remembers
the connections woven, little eggs
along the message line.

I remember giving dinosaurs
to the tall unfolded ferns to entertain them.
And immortality to the cockroach.
I remember the birthday of the first
flower, and the death of so many furry

animals and kinds of people, and a star
that fell. I remember a continent
of green
green wands of grass
burning into the knees of
buffalo queens, a landlocked
ocean of fire. Replaced by the
picket fence. Almost equally complex.
Sky scrapers like spikes.
But that's another song.
And I am the Queen of Wands
who burns, who glows, who webs
the message strands,
who stands, who always will.

I remember the birthday of the first
flower, and the death of so many furry
animals and kinds of people, and a star
that fell. I remember a continent
of green
green wands of grass
burning into the knees of
buffalo queens, a landlocked
ocean of fire. Replaced by the
picket fence. Almost equally complex.
Skyscrapers like spikes.
But that's another song.
And I am the Queen of Wands
who burns, who glows, who webs
the message strands,
who stands, who always will.

SUSAN GRIFFIN

~~~~~~

The Great Mother

I was walking in
Tilden Park
ready to
throw myself
down a ravine
when suddenly
from a helicopter
parachuted
The Great Mother.
"Hello," she said,
and immediately
surrounded me in an aura
of light and comfort. "Never,
again," she sang,
"will you walk
alone and in anguish."
I was
thrilled and
about to express my
amazement when
suddenly she backed off
and put up her hand,
"Don't ask!"—she smiled—
"I know your every thought

before you even
open your mouth. You
wanted to know
why didn't I come before?"
I opened my mouth to say
no, but
before I could speak she
answered.
"In wanting to
throw yourself
down the ravine
your anguish was so
deep that
suddenly I knew you
truly needed me," she said, and
her hair fanned out
green the color
of the oak
tree growing from the ravine, so
I wanted to say "Yes, but
there were other times I've
wanted to throw myself down
other ravines,"
still, afraid to offend her,
I remained silent.
"I know what your
silence means,"
she said.
"You are asking if
I *am* the Great Mother
all powerful
able to answer all
cries of anguish in all
parks, private and public places
why did I let the anguish
exist in the first place?"
I said nothing.
"A good question," she said.
"And you must already know

the answer, it is"—she
gestured gracefully with
a swanlike movement of her enormous
sari billowing in the wind—
"One of my mysteries."
I gaped.
"You must also wonder,"
she went on,
looking now to the skies,
"If I am so
kind
just
and all-knowing
hearing every cry
how can I answer
the 11 million eight hundred
and forty-three
cries of truly significant
anguish,
that come to me
every five minutes,
on a statistical average."
I shrugged my shoulders.
"Because," she said,
"*that* is another mystery."
She went on.
"The Great Mother
takes a multitude
of shapes in a multitude
of places
breast, womb, heart
chicken soup, Red Cross
nurse, milk of human
kindness, security blanket,
these are but
signs of my eternal
hovering presence
but only do I
materialize when

a true seeker . . ."
"Just a moment," I
said
beginning
to catch my breath
but then she
began to fade.
"I am," I said,
and then she disappeared al-
together
and I whispered to
myself filled with
awe, "I am
an
atheist."

This Earth

WHAT SHE IS TO ME
One should identify oneslf with the universe itself. Everything that
is less than the universe is subjected to suffering . . .
        SIMONE WEIL, *Notebooks*

As I go into her, she pierces my heart. As I penetrate further, she unveils
me. When I have reached her center, I am weeping openly. I have known her
all my life, yet she reveals stories to me, and these stories are revelations and
I am transformed. Each time I go to her I am born like this. Her renewal washes
over me endlessly, her wounds caress me; I become aware of all that has come
between us, of the noise between us, the blindness, of something sleeping
between us. Now my body reaches out to her. They speak effortlessly, and I
learn at no instant does she fail me in her presence. She is as delicate as I am;
I know her sentience; I feel her pain and my own pain comes into me, and my
own pain grows large and I grasp this pain with my hands, and I open my
mouth to this pain, I taste, I know, and I know why she goes on, under great
weight, with this great thirst, in drought, in starvation, with intelligence in

every act does she survive disaster. This earth is my sister; I love her daily grace, her silent daring, and how loved I am *how we admire this strength in each other, all that we have lost, all that we have suffered, all that we know: we are stunned by this beauty,* and I do not forget what she is to me, what I am to her.

Our Mother

At the center of the earth there is a mother.
If any of us who are her children choose to die
she feels a grief like a wound deeper
than any of us can imagine.
She puts her hands to her face
like this: her palms open.
Put them there like she does.
Her fingers press into her eyes.
Do that, too.
She tries to howl.
Some of us have decided
this mother cannot hear all of us
in our desperate wishes.
Here, in this time,
our hearts have been cut into small chambers
like ration cards
and we can no longer imagine every
morsel nor each tiny
thought at once,
as *she* still can.
This is normal,
she tries to tell us,
but we don't listen.
Sometimes someone has a faint memory
of all this, and
she suffers.
She is wrong to imagine

she suffers alone.
Do you think we are not all hearing and speaking
at the same time?
Our mother is somber.
She is thinking.
She puts her big ear
against the sky
to comfort herself.
Do this. She calls to us,
Do this.

JOY HARJO

～～～～～～～～～～～～～～～～～～～～～～～～～～～～～～

Remember

Remember the sky that you were born under,
know each of the star's stories.
Remember the moon, know who she is. I met her
in a bar once in Iowa City.
Remember the sun's birth at dawn, that is the
strongest point of time. Remember sundown
and the giving away to night.
Remember your birth, how your mother struggled
to give you form and breath. You are evidence of
her life, and her mother's, and hers.
Remember your father, his hands cradling
your mother's flesh, and maybe her heart, too
and maybe not.
He is your life, also.
Remember the earth whose skin you are.
Red earth yellow earth white earth brown earth
black earth we are earth.
Remember the plants, trees, animal life who all have their
tribes, their families, their histories, too. Talk to them,
listen to them. They are alive poems.
Remember the wind. Remember her voice. She knows the
origin of this universe. I heard her singing Kiowa war
dance songs at the corner of Fourth and Central once.
Remember that you are all people and that all people

are you.
Remember that you are this universe and that this
universe is you.
Remember that all is in motion, is growing, is you.
Remember that language comes from this.
Remember the dance that language is, that life is.
Remember
to remember.

White Bear

She begins to board the flight
        to Albuquerque. Late night.
But stops in the corrugated tunnel,
        a space between leaving and staying,
where the night sky catches

                her whole life

she has felt like a woman
        balancing on a wooden nickle heart
approaching herself from here to
        there, Tulsa or New York
with knives or corn meal.

The last flight someone talked
        about how coming from Seattle
the pilot flew a circle
        over Mt. St. Helens; she sat
quiet. (But had seen the eruption
        as the earth beginning
to come apart, as in birth
        out of violence.)

She watches the yellow lights
    of towns below the airplane flicker,
fade and fall backwards. Somewhere,
    she dreamed, there is the white bear
moving down from the north, motioning her paws
    like a long arctic night, that kind
of circle and the whole world balanced in
    between carved of ebony and ice

        oh so hard

the clear black nights
    like her daughter's eyes, and the white
bear moon, cupped like an ivory rocking
cradle, tipping back it could go
either way
        all darkness
                is open to all light.

Grace

I think of Wind and her wild ways the year we had nothing to lose and lost
it anyway in the cursed country of the fox. We still talk about that winter,
how the cold froze imaginary buffalo on the stuffed horizon of snowbanks.
The haunting voices of the starved and mutilated broken fences, crashed
our thermostat dreams, and we couldn't stand it one more time. So once
again we lost a winter in stubborn memory, walked through cheap
apartment walls, skated through fields of ghosts into a town that never
wanted us, in the epic search for grace.

Like Coyote, like Rabbit we could not contain our terror and clowned our
way through a season of false midnights. We had to swallow that town
with laughter, so it would go down easy as honey. And one morning as the
sun struggled to break ice, and our dreams had found us with coffee and
pancakes in a truckstop along highway eighty; we found grace.

I could say grace was a woman with time on her hands, or a white buffalo escaped from memory. But in that dingy light it was a promise of balance. We once again understood the talk of animals, and spring was lean and hungry with the hope of children and corn.

I would like to say, with grace, we picked ourselves up and walked into the spring thaw. We didn't; the next season was worse. You went home to Leech Lake to work with the tribe and I went south. And Wind, I am still crazy. I know there is something larger than the memory of a dispossessed people. We have seen it.

The Book of Myths

When I entered the book of myths
                    in your sandalwood room on the granite island,
    I did not ask for a way out.
This is not the century for false pregnancy
                    in these times when myths
                                have taken to the streets.
There is no more imagination, we are in it now, girl.
    We traveled the stolen island of Manhattan
                in a tongue of wind off the Atlantic
        shaking our shells, in our mad skins.
I did not tell you when I saw Rabbit sobbing and laughing
                            as he shook his dangerous bag of tricks
            into the mutiny world on that street outside Hunter.
Out came you and I blinking our eyes once more, entwined in our loves
        and hates as we set off to recognize the sweet
and bitter gods who walk beside us,   whisper madness
in our invisible ears any ordinary day.
    I have fallen in love a thousand times over, every day is a common
miracle of salt roses, of fire in the prophecy wind, and now and then
            I taste the newborn blood in my daughter's
                silk hair, as if she were not nearly a woman
        brown and electric in her nearly woman self.

There is a Helen in every language; in American her name is Marilyn
                    but in my subversive country,
          she is dark earth and round and full of names
dressed in bodies of women
          who enter and leave the knife wounds of this terrifyingly
beautiful land;
                    we call ourselves ripe, and pine tree and woman.
          In the book of myths that fell open in your room of unicorns
I did not imagine the fiery goddess in the middle of the island.
She is a sweet trick of flame,
                    had everyone dancing, laughing and telling the stories
that unglue the talking spirit from the pages.
When the dawn light came on through the windows,
                    I understood how my bones would one day
          stand up, brush off the lovely skin like a satin blouse
and dance with foolish grace to heaven.

JANA HARRIS

Beneath the Pole of Proud Raven

She said, Creek Daughter
give me your gray gray hair,
creek daughter, give me
the glacier water,
— gray hair, cold water —
give me their child, creek daughter
give me the fish, creek daughter
give me your gray gray hair

She said, Fish
give me your silver skin, fish
give me your silver silver skin
give me your silver salmon skin
fish, give me your skin

She said, Loon
give me your noise, loon
give me your high pitched crazed call,
give me your loon-call echoing
off the island rocks, loon
give me your noise, loon
give me your noise

She said, Wolf
tired wolf, tired swimming wolf
give me your claws, tired wolf
give me your claws

She said, Crow
give me your coat, crow
give me your raven down coat
give me your coat like night,
crow, give me the night, crow
give me your coat

She said, Woman
give me the fog, woman
give me the fog, give me
the spruce-root hat where
you've hidden the fog
woman, give me the fog

She said, Coals
give me the fire spirit, coals
give me your pitch-stick smell,
give me your spruce-gum smoke
coals, give me the fire spirit

She said, Whale
give me your bones, blackfin
give me their slopes and hills,
bring me the mountains, whale
give me your bones

She said, Creek Daughter
give me your gray gray hair
give me the glacier water
She said, Fish
give me your silver silver skin
She said, Loon
give me your noise, loon
She said, Wolf

tired swimming wolf
give me your claws
She said, Crow
give me your coat like night
She said, Woman
give me the fog
She said, Coals
give me the fire spirit
She said, Whale
give me your bones, blackfin
bring me the mountains

She said,
I am the glacier
She said,
I am the fish
She said,
I am the loon
She said,
I am the wolf
She said,
I am the night
She said,
I am the fog
She said,
I am the fire
She said,
I am the mountain
She said,
I am the power
She said,
I am the earth
She said,

Beware

ERICA HELM

The Creation Songs of Eurynome

I   *Eurynome Divides Chaos*

In the beginning there was only
In the beginning there was only chaos
coiled serpent in a cold darkness.
In the beginning there was only
cold and tangled chaos and the dark.

The only sound that could be heard
was my breath skirling through
the twisted no-thing where it all began.
The only heat was the hot breath
steaming in my breast.

       These are the first words of Eurynome
       maker of all and every.
       These are the first words
       before the one and the two, before the three,
       before the four from which all things came.

I seized hold of the two tails of chaos;
the one and the two twined together
in forever's grasp —

seized hold of forever
and rent chaos in two.

The first limb of chaos
was fluid and smooth; light to hold.
I spread it above and called it Sky.
The second limb was fluid and heavy.
I released it below and called it the Sea.

II   *Eurynome Creates Her Consort Ophion*

I danced along the sea;
surging, lifting, falling back.
Rippling froth caressed my knees.
The watery sky opened where I danced.
Waves swelled up and rose behind me.

Waves rolled apart as I cleaved the sea.
Spray pelted the air — I reeled faster and harder
plowing deep furrows where water meets air!
Wind whirled along the waves behind me,
whipped and furled my hair!

Sucking my hair to its greedy maw,
the wind licked my hips and thighs;
lashed up into my groin.
I seized hold of the wind
and clasped it firmly to my breast.

I pressed it to my breasts and thighs —
twisted it round, kneaded and spiraled,
stirred and braided. I shook and compressed the wind,
consumed and subsumed him. I apprehended his spirit,
with my soul. Striving wrought substance: wind became flesh.

He entered me— coiled round me,
enclosed and engulfed me in scaly folds.

I became a dove and soared down to him.
He became a serpent, rising up to me:
entering me, entwining me, entering me, entwining me

Ophion, my Ophion.

III *Eurynome Births the Egg of the Universe*

I grew great with the generation of our seed —
swelled ripe with the fruits of our bond.
I spread my dove wings and cried.
Spasms churned through me.
The fists of chaos tore my flesh.

The Egg of the Universe, thrust of my womb,
floated on the water.
"Open!" I cried, "Let me see what is born!
Open! Let me see what is born! "
But the shell did not yield to entreaties or blows.

"Ophion!" I cried, "Coil round the egg! Rend it in two!
Coil round, rend it in two!"
The great serpent of the wind coiled round —
One, two, three — my consort coiled round .
"Now squeeze tightly!" but the egg held firm.

"Ophion! Coil round again!"
My consort wrapped the egg; four, five, six,
constricted, yet nothing gave .
"Ophion! You have one length left!
Coil round again and squeeze!"

I spread my dove wings and cried,
"Open let me see what is born !"
The great serpent of the wind coiled round.
The seventh time the serpent wound, the world-egg cracked in two.
The seventh time the serpent wound, the world egg cracked in two.

IV *The Egg of the Universe Hatches All Things*

The egg of the universe fell open;
two perfect, pearly bowls afloat on the sea .
The stars flew out first and scattered like seeds.
The moon floated to center sky
shedding infinite ghostly petals on the sea.

The shameless sun shot out and blinded the sky.
Then the planets rose up and found their places.
The earth spilled out with its mountains and trees,
its valleys, plains and rivers .
Eurynome set foot upon earth. "It is good," said the mother of all things.

Eurynome and Ophion resided on Olympus —
savored the fragrant earth below,
adored the brilliant sky, sweet honey and riversong.
The mother of all things basked
in the sublime light of creation.

V *Eurynome Banishes Ophion and Completes Creation*

He grew bored, my Ophion;
bored with beauty, bored with drone of bee to flower,
humming bird to fuchsia,
stag to hind, flower to fruit,
fruit to harvest, harvest to seed, seed to earth and round.

He wished more for himself than to be part of the round.
He claimed ownership, authorship; at first whispering
to bird and brute, "Creation is mine,"
and then shouting from hilltops, "I am Ophion:
Creator of all and every, Maker of all things! "

I, Eurynome, Separator of the limbs of chaos,
Maker of wind, Seizor of the serpent, Mother of the universe,
have no patience for braggarts or plagiarizing fools.
I kicked my consort in the teeth and banished him
to a pit at the edge of the world, where he lies still.

I returned to Olympus, gazed out upon creation
and for the first time noticed: something was missing.
In those early days, small creatures were coupled
but the great eternal things stood alone. I ruled alone!
The solitary planets in their courses rolled sterile across the sky.

This was when I understood and out of longing, completed creation.
I made a queen and a king to rule each planet:
each planetary power, a meld of poles, a union.
She-ness penetrating mind, he-ness enveloping body.
Mother seed to father, father seed to mother.

The male egg containing, gestating female seed,
imbuing, entwining, engulfing, entwining.
Later stories say the planets are male, except Venus and the moon.
This is not true! I placed a king and queen in each planet
to rule in harmonic dissonance, tender disagreement, bold union.

      These are the words of Eurynome,
      Separator of the one and the two,
      Maker of the three,
      Mother of the four
      from which all things came.

      This is how the first pairs came to be—
      the She and the He, the He and the She,
      engulfed and entwined, queen and king;
      how she hid them in each other
      how she hid them in each other.

LINDA HOGAN

Desert

This is the earth,
skin stretched bare
like a woman who teaches her daughters to plant,
leaving the ants in their places,
the spiders in theirs.
She teaches them to turn the soil
one grain at a time.
They plant so carefully
seeds grow from their hands.

When they learn to weave
it is lace they make,
the white spines of a cactus,
backbone,
a lace containing the heat of sun
and night's bare moon.
The oldest child's sorrow song woven
so much like the wind.

This is the forest turned to sand
but it goes on.
Insects drink moisture
off their own bodies.
The shriveled winter cactus,

one drop of water
raises it from dry sand.
That is what I teach my daughters,
that we are women,
a hundred miles of green
wills itself out of our skin.
The red sky ends at our feet
and the earth begins at our heads.

Tiva's Tapestry: La Llorona

White-haired woman of winter,
la Llorona
with the river's black
unraveling
drowned children from her hands.

At night frozen leaves
rustle the sound of her skirt.
Listen and wind comes spinning
her song from the burning eyes of animals
from the owl
whose eyes look straight ahead.
She comes dragging
the dark river
a ghost on fire
for children she held
under water.

Stars are embroidered on the dark.
Long shadows, long like rivers
I am sewing
shut the doors
filling the windows in with light.
This needle pierces a thousand kisses

and rage
the shape of a woman.
I light this house,
sprinkle salt on my sleeping child
so dreams won't fly her into the night.

These fingers have sewn a darkness
and flying away
on the white hair growing
on the awful tapestry of sky
just one of the mothers
among the downward circling stars.

Morning: The World in the Lake

Beneath each black duck
another swims,
shadow
joined to blood and flesh.

There's a world beneath this one.
The red-winged blackbird calls
its silent comrade down below.

The world rises
and descends
in the black eyes of a bird,
its crescent of fire
crossing lake and sky,
its breast turning up on water.

The sun burns behind dark mountains.

My daughter rises at water's edge.
Her face lies down on water

and the bird flies through her.
The world falls
into her skin
down to the world beneath,
the fiery leap of a fish
falling into itself.

And then it rises, the blackbird
above the world's geography of light and dark
and we are there, living
in that revealed sliver of red
living in the black
something of feathers,
daughters, all of us,
who would sleep as if reflected
alongside our mothers,
the mothers of angels and shadows,
the helix and spiral of centuries
twisting inside.
The radiant ones are burning
beneath this world.
They rise up
the quenching water.

November

The sun climbs down
the dried out ladders of corn.
Its red fire walks down the rows.
Dry corn sings, *Shh, Shh.*

The old sky woman has opened her cape
to show off the red inside
like burning hearts
holy people enter.

I will walk with her.
We are both burning.
We walk in the field of dry corn
where birds are busy gleaning.

The corn says, *Shh.*
I walk beside the pens holding animals.
The old woman sun rises,
red, on the backs of small pigs.

She rides the old sow
down on her knees in mud.
Her prayers do not save her.
Her many teats do not save her.

I won't think of the butcher walking away
with blood on his shoes,
red footprints of fire. In them
the sow walks away from her own death.

The sun rides the old sow
like an orange bird on its back.
God save the queen.
Her castle rises in the sky and crumbles.

She has horses the color of wine.
The little burgundy one
burns and watches while I walk.
The rusty calves watch with dark eyes.

The corn says, *Shh,*
and birds beat the red air
like a dusty rug. They sing
God save the queen.

My hair burns down my shoulders.
I walk. I will not think we are blood sacrifices.
No, I will not watch the ring-necked pheasant
running into the field of skeletal corn.

64 — Linda Hogan

I will walk into the sun.
Her red mesas are burning
in the distance.
I will enter them. I will walk into that stone,

walk into the sun
away from night rising up the other side of earth.
There are sounds in the cornfield,
Shh. Shh.

First Light

In early morning
I forget I'm in this world
with crooked chiefs
who make federal deals.

In the first light
I remember who rewards me for living, not bosses
but singing birds and blue sky.

I know I can bathe and stretch,
make jewelry and love
the witch and wise woman
living inside, needing to be silenced
and put at rest for work's long day.

In the first light
I offer cornmeal
and tobacco.
I say hello to those who came before me, and to birds
under the eaves,
and budding plants.

I know the old ones are here.
And every morning I remember the song
about how buffalo left through a hole in the sky
and how the grandmothers look out from those holes
watching over us
from there and from there.

Scorpion

In the old days
she was a god
living in dark furrows
of earth-smelling earth,
that woman the stars were named for.

She was a god
living in the corn husk and silk world that was torn open.

She was sister to the heat waves
rising up southern nights.
Don't come close!
Crony of red sky, she lived
beneath stones,
those progeny of stars
with their long waiting
for what?

Tonight she is exiled to cupboards and stoops.
Even the stars and moon
have fallen
over summer's edge,
burning like razed towns
charred heart and soul
to earth.

Surrounded by flames
she wants to sting herself to death.
But sister,
we've all been surrounded
with no escape
from mean fire
and life or death,
and there's a whole continent
in this ring of fire,
breaking,
breaking into itself
with stinger and beak,
stopping its own watched heart,
that prehistoric heart
that remembers the gods
of furrow and corn.

That scorpion life
exiled to brown shoes and porches
knows something is wrong.
She is crawling
out the shoe,
that danger to bony feet.
Even the elements are at war.
I see,
I see
in the old days
we were all gods,
even the foot and its leather.
We were all gods
of shelter,
all this fiery life burning like wood,
and it does.

It Must Be

I am an old woman
whose skin looks young
though I ache
and have heard the gravediggers call me
by name.

The pathologists come
with their forceps and gowns.
It must be a disease, they say,
it must be.

It must be, they say
over there in the joints
that her grandmothers refuse to bend
one more time
though her face smiles at the administrators
taking reports.

The doctors come
with their white coats and masks.
It must be
her heart, let us cut her open with knives.

Doctor, did you hear the singing in my heart?
Or find the broken-off love, the lost brother?
Surely you witnessed all the old women
who live in the young house of this body
and how they are full of black wool and clipped nails.

They make me carry on
under my jeans and sweater,
traditions and complaints about the sad
state of the nation.

They have big teeth
for biting through leather and birch bark
and lies
about the world.

They have garlic in their pockets
to protect us from the government.

The nurses arrive with pink nails
and the odor of smoke. They arrive
from lifting the hips of old men
as if they were not old men.

One of the old women inside
lashes out at the nurses
and all who remain girls,
and at bankers and scholars.
But despite that old woman,
there are days I see my girlish hands
and wonder which banker owns them
and there are nights I watch the wrong face
in the mirror, and afternoons
I hold that face down to the floor by its neck
with those banker's hands,
those scholar's hands
that wish to silence the old woman inside
who tells the truth
and how it must be.

And there are days
the old women gossip and sing,
offering gifts of red cloth and cornbread
to one another.
On those days I love the ancestors
in and around me,
the mothers of trees and deer
and harvests, and that crazy one
in her nightgown
baring herself to the world,
daring the psychiatrists to come
with their couches and theories and rats.
On those days the oldest one is there,
taking stock
in all her shining
and with open hands.

CAROLYN KIZER

Hera, Hung from the Sky

I hang by my heels from the sky.
The sun, exploded at last,
Hammered his wrath to chains
Forged for my lightest bones.
Once I was warmed to my ears,
Kept close; now blind with fire !
What a child, taking heat for delight
So simply ! Scorched within,
I still burn as I swing,
A pendulum kicking the night,
An alarum at dawn, I deflect
The passage of birds, ring down
The bannering rain. I indict
This body, its ruses, games,
Its plot to unseat the sun.
I pitted my feminine weight
Against God, his terrible throne.
From the great dome of despair,
I groan, I swing, I swing
In unconstellated air.

I had shared a sovereign cloud:
The lesser, the shadowy twin
To my lord. All woman and weight

Of connubial love that sings
Within the cabinet's close
And embracing intimacy.
I threw it all to the skies
In an instant of power, poise—
Arrogant, flushed with his love,
His condescending praise;
From envy of shine and blaze,
Mad, but beautifully mad,
Hypnotized by the gaze
Of self into self, the dream
That woman was great as man—
As humid, as blown with fame,
So great I seemed to be !
I threw myself to the skies
And the sky has cast me down.
I have lost the war of the air:
Half-strangled in my hair,
I dangle, drowned in fire.

Persephone Pauses

The lengthened shadow of my hand
Holding a letter from a friend
Tells time: the sun descends again.
So long, so late the light has shone.
Since rising, we have shone with ease:
Perhaps not happiness, but still
A certain comfort from the trees
Whose crests of leaves droop down in tiers,
Their warm trunks veiled by aspen hair,
Their honeyed limbs, the loosened earth
About the roots; while flowers recline
In dusty gardens, rest on weeds,
Those emblems of a passing year.

So be it ! As I turn, my train
Is plucked by spikes of summer grass.
No clutch of summer holds me here.
I know, I know. I've gone before.
I glance to my accustomed glass,
The shallow pond, but films of slime
Waver across it, suck the verge
Where blunted marsh frond cuts the air.
But as I stare, the slime divides
Like curtains of old green velour:

I gaze into my gaze once more,
Still veiled in foam. But then, the grim
Tragedian from the other shore
Draws near my shade. Beneath the brim,
In motions formal and austere,

We circle, measure, heel to hem.
He proffers me an iron plate
Of seedy fruit, to match my mouth.
My form encased in some dark stuff
He has bedizened, keeps me hid
Save for that quivering oval, turned
Half-moon, away, away from him
And that excitement of his taste
He suffers, from my flesh withdrawn.

But this unwilling touch of lust
Has moved some gentle part of me
That sleeps in solstice, wakes to dream
Where streams of light and winter join.
He knows me then; I only know
A darkened cheek, a sidelong lower,
My nerves dissolving in the gleam
Of night's theatrical desire,
As always, when antagonists
Are cast into the sensual
Abysses, from a failing will.
This is my dolor, and my dower.

Come then, sweet Hell ! I'll name you once
To stir the grasses, rock the pool,
And move the leaves before they fall.
I cast my letter to the breeze
Where paper wings will sprout, and bear
It on to that high messenger
Of sky, who lately dropped it here,
Reminding me, as I decline,
That half my life is spent in light.
I cast my spirit to the air,
But cast it. Summertime, goodnight!

Semele Recycled

After you left me forever
I was broken into pieces,
and all the pieces flung into the river.
Then the legs crawled ashore
and aimlessly wandered the dusty cow-track.
They became, for awhile, a simple roadside shrine:
A tiny table set up between the thighs
held a dusty candle, weed and fieldflower chains
placed reverently there by children and old women.
My knees were hung with tin triangular medals
to cure all forms of hysterical disease.

After I died forever in the river,
my torso floated, bloated in the stream,
catching on logs or stones among the eddies.
White water foamed around it, then dislodged it;
after a whirlwind trip it bumped ashore.
A grizzled old man who scavenged along the banks
had already rescued my arms and put them by,
knowing everything has its uses, sooner or later.

When he found my torso, he called it his canoe,
and, using my arms as paddles,
he rowed me up and down the scummy river.
When catfish nibbled my fingers he scooped them up,
and blessed his re-usable bait.
Clumsy but serviceable, that canoe!
The trail of blood that was its wake
attracted the carp and eels, and the river turtle,
easily landed, dazed by my tasty red.

A young lad found my head among the rushes
and placed it on a dry stone.
He carefully combed my hair with a bit of shell
and set small offering before it
which the birds and rats obligingly stole at night,
so it seemed I ate.
And the breeze wound through my mouth and empty sockets
so my lungs would sigh, and my dead tongue mutter.
Attached to my throat like a sacred necklace
was a circlet of small snails.
Soon the villagers came to consult my oracular head
with its waterweed crown.
Seers found occupation, interpreting sighs,
and their papyrus rolls accumulated.

Meanwhile, young boys retrieved my eyes
they used for marbles in a simple game
—till somebody's pretty sister snatched at them
and set them, for luck, in her bridal diadem.
Poor girl ! When her future groom caught sight of her,
all eyes, he crossed himself in horror,
and stumbled away in haste
through her dowered meadows.

When then of my heart and organs,
my sacred slit
which loved you best of all?
They were caught in a fisherman's net
and tossed at night into a pen for swine.

But they shone so by moonlight that the sows stampeded,
trampled each other in fear, to get away.
And the fisherman's wife, who had 13 living children
and was contemptuous of holy love,
raked the rest of me onto the compost heap.

Then in their various places and helpful functions,
the altar, oracle, offal, canoe and oars
learned the wild rumor of your return.
The altar leapt up, and ran to the canoe,
scattering candle grease and wilted grasses.
Arms sprang to their sockets, blind hands with nibbled nails
groped their way, aided by loud lamentation,
to the bed of the bride, snatched up those unlucky eyes
from her discarded veil and diadem,
and rammed them home. O what a bright day it was !
This empty body danced on the river bank.
Hollow, it called and searched among the fields
for those parts that steamed and simmered in the sun,
and never would have found them.

But then your great voice rang out under the skies
my name !—and all those private names
for the parts and places that had loved you best.
And they stirred in their nest of hay and dung.
The distraught old ladies chasing their lost altar,
and the seers pursuing my skull, their lost employment,
and the tumbling boys, who wanted the magic marbles,
and the runaway groom, and the fisherman's 13 children
set up such a clamor, with their cries of "Miracle!"
that our two bodies met like a thunderclap
in mid-day; right at the corner of that wretched field
with its broken fenceposts and startled, skinny cattle.
We fell in a heap on the compost heap
and all our loving parts made love at once,
while the bystanders cheered and prayed and hid their eyes
and then went decently about their business.

And here it is, moonlight again; we've bathed in the river
and are sweet and wholesome once more.
We kneel side-by-side in the sand;
we worship each other in whispers.
But the inner parts remember fermenting hay,
the comfortable odor of dung, the animal incense,
and passion, its bloody labor,
its birth and rebirth and decay.

MARY NORBERT KORTE

Rain to River to The Sea

Dear Rose
            rain speaks each
water mouths a giant mumbling
and thunder sounds a huge systolic beat
behind the eyes as I grow   as I get on
days are short   sun sets in a loud
crash   lightning strikes more places by chance
by chance we have come to know there are ways
to see the startracks on every thing   we touch
explosions of light at the center of storm
and learn   and learn that   and learn this

songs in the howling of water are the notes
our mothers   wept   the cries of woods   the thick
laying down of fog in hollow drums
courses through us   the women who know
Isis knew it   Demeter knew that blood
and Kali grew blood from a language
laid against the silent dew

we trace the notes of our breast-fed cries
along the spinebacks of wild grasses
bent by wind and the force of growing we sing

the piercing watersongs our mothers made
to feed us   we sing   songs the Mother makes
for ever   holding   holding our selves
in the long embrace of the sea

This Room Of Trees & Moving Earth
This Room Where No One Knows How Sky Begins

Something in us is angry at the rain
the cat stalks at the window angry the
angry damp blotch on his shoulder he licks
my wrist insistent with the anger of the little
girl who screams   *come back come back*
to her father in the dark woods
even music does not fill the inside
of the bowl that rain upends on us
the huge lonely sigh breathes in the house
I hear him whine outside the dog who
lived a while with me and went away
in the rain lying quiet in the rain
and all the rain   and all there is to do
and argue   with this free blood
we shed in every death   we shed
in every rain

          in this forest   in the end
it is the rain that is the power   not love
nor insects nor death nor violent blossoms
throwing themselves against weak sun on the ridge
in the ecstasy of its blind shout
rain begins to pull on every thing tears
and paths its way through the bones
to a light that has stricken every creature down
the cruel light the cruel
dancing light dancing of rain

stuns us strips us feeds on us
carries into brambles stiff with flood
beats us down to the real earth moving
restlessly threaded with its force

and something in us is angry at the rain
the birds   the birds that they should caw
and kek and cry each other off
that our backs should set awry
that so much beauty should enthrone itself on blood
that so much life should rage itself to death
that so much blood should burn unheeded by the rain

the rain is Mother Kali   her lust
for us in the woods grows a giant lungs
we live in the heave and whoosh of those
bellows swimming and gasping for light
so we learn to suckle from inside her breast
and feed upon our blood and the blood
of unsettled rocks the blood of trees
and learn to let the dog
die softly in the woods and let bracken
poke its fiddlehead between the ribs
and let the great dog jaw grow moss
and the eye   sockets ringed with lichen lie
inward   secret   filled with her   with her rain
                                        with rain

and let the rain make us leaf and branch   scatter us
bone and veins on trillium   kingfisher   adder's tongue
bring us to the gills we grew once and sloughed
in the slow swim toward a knife of light
let the rain pool and grow within our tight skin
squeeze out warm through fists
rain put itself in   in the center   where is
the great dream down the carrying the carrying rain

rain carry us on spring and creek and river to the sea

The Cat

someone said this was the ugliest cat
she had ever seen   it's true
the crossed eyes wander into spiderwebs
corner the reincarnation of a grumpy surprise
soft spotted anger deposes itself   on a chair
                                                        on a shelf
                                                        on the bed

but sometimes she becomes incandescent
along water way beyond   crossing beargrass
she becomes a torch in the woods
eyes and fur stand burning
as midnight weeds wailing in sun
there glows on her head
a hot redburning eye intense as ruby
in the fur she speaks from a place
of rumoured power   a place
just out the corner of watching
and she guards her place   her light
guards its way slowly through trees
in woods that are not kind to animals
she stalks riverfog   pulls on that most
fragile of threads the secret path
that takes her to my room

death is picturesque here in the woods not kind
dead trees around piled in river voices
the dead thrive and are busy and such as
the cat sees she stiffens riding her hairs
every hair of the head numbered
eyes the center of lush burning
the bird drunk   flutters in the house
vines of fire climb the walls of the house roar
at the stars so cold in this drought year
the ground breaks of it

Hecate cries through a hole in the trees
and the cat cries   the cat sings
the cat sings of fire of lupine
the cat sings of lupine nights sleeping
                    in the beds of deer

MERIDEL LE SUEUR

Hush, My Little Grandmother

Hush, my little grandmother
I am a woman come to speak for you.
I am a woman speaking for us all
From the tongue of dust and fire
From the bowl of bitter smoke.
This is a song for strength and power.
Water is pouring
                water is running,
The drouthy blooms,
It is coming out pouring in bloom of day.
Let us all go down there and bathe in the water.
The water is coming on the four paths of the eagles.
Let us all, of many colors, go down where the waters come
Calling   calling to us   in rivers of wind and blood.
We are floods
                We are Apache plumes
We are the brave cacti's rosy blossom,
Forgetting the thorns and the dry
We are glut of a stong thrust grandmother.
Hush   hush my little root
My empty pod,
Hush   hush my little grandmother,

I am a woman come to speak
in tongues of dust and fire,
Woman bowled
and filled with pollen.

Behold This and Always Love It

O my daughters
My bowl is full of sweet grass,
I approach in my best buckskin,
I travel the path of the people
Behold me!
The white buffalo woman brings the
sacred pipe of vision.
Standing on the hill behold me
Coming coming coming
Over the prairie breast I come
sacred,
Covered by a cloud of flowers.
Behold what you see, my grandchildren
Behold this
And always love it.

She moves   she moves   all moves to her.
In the bowl   the basket   the earth bowl
She is adorned in the middle country
She appears in the crops of Kansas.
In Oklahoma brothels,
In erupting volcanoes,
At the peyote ceremony of birds.
In the hell holes and the heavenly meadows
she appears.
From far away she is coming   coming
From all the roads she is coming   coming.
They are gathering.   They are coming.

The ancients are coming with the children.
From far away they are coming   incessantly
                                    coming.

Send out a crier, she says
                    I want to talk to the people.
Listen   Listen   while you are walking
All is upon the earth and all is sacred.

Rites of Ancient Ripening

I am luminous with age
In my lap I hold the valley.
I see on the horizon what has been taken
What is gone   lies prone   fleshless.
In my breast I hold the middle valley
The corn kernels cry to me in the fields
                    Take us home.
Like corn I cry in the last sunset
Gleam like plums.
                    My bones shine in fever
Smoked with the fires of age.
Herbal, I contain the final juice,
Shadow, I crouch in the ash
                    never breaking to fire.
Winter iron bough
                    unseen my buds,
Hanging close I live in the beloved bone
Speaking in the marrow
                    alive in green memory.
The light was brighter then.
Now spiders creep at my eyes' edge.
I peek between my fingers
                    at my fathers' dust.
The old stones have been taken away

there is no path.
The fathering fields are gone.
The wind is stronger than it used to be.
My stone feet far below me grip the dust.
I run and crouch in corners with thin dogs.
I tie myself to the children like a kite.
I fall and burst beneath the sacred human tree.
Release my seed and let me fall.
Toward the shadow of the great earth
                    let me fall.
Without child or man
              I turn   I fall.
Into shadows,
           the dancers are gone.
My salted pelt stirs at the final warmth
Pound me death
           stretch and tan me death
Hang me up, ancestral shield
           against the dark.

Burn and bright and take me quick.
Pod and light me into dark.

Are those flies or bats or mother eagles?
I shrink   I cringe
Trees tilt upon me like young men.
The bowl I made I cannot lift.
All is running past me.
The earth tilts and tums over me.
I am shrinking
        and lean against the warm walls of old summers.
With knees and chin I grip the dark
Swim out the shores of night in old meadows.
Remember   buffalo hunts
Great hunters returning
Councils of the fathers to be fed
Round sacred fires.
The faces of profound deer who
                    gave themselves for food.
We faced the east the golden pollened

86 — Meridel Le Sueur

     sacrifice of brothers.
The little seeds of my children
     with faces of mothers and fathers
Fold in my flesh
     in future summers.
My body a canoe turning to stone
Moves among the bursting flowers of memory
Through the meadows of flowers and food,
I float and wave to my grandchildren in the
Tepis of many fires
     In the winter of the many slain
I hear the moaning.
I ground my corn daily
In my pestle many children
Summer grasses in my daughters
Strength and fathers in my sons
All was ground in the bodies bowl
  corn died to bread
    woman to child
     deer to the hunters.
Sires of our people
Wombs of mothering night
Guardian mothers of the corn
Hill borne torrents of the plains
Sing all grinding songs
 of healing herbs
Many tasselled summers
   Flower in my old bones
   Now.
Ceremonials of water and fire
Lodge me in the deep earth
 grind my harvested seed.
The rites of ancient ripening
Make my flesh plume
And summer winds stir in my smoked bowl.
Do not look for me till I return
    rot of greater summers
Struck from fire and dark,
Mother struck to future child.

Unbud me now
Unfurl me now
Flesh and fire
             burn
                  requicken
                        Death.

Let the Bird of Earth, Fly!

I send my voice of sorrow
        calling calling
My bowl is full of grief
            and the wind is up.
Thanks, all the people are crying
Behold and listen!
All is grown here
            where the sun goes down,
The world within our hands
            flies upward like a bird.
All that moves rejoices.
Approach each other as relatives
I give you corn
        I give you love
He he eyee eyee
Let the bird of the earth loose,
        dove from the dark ark.
Flood out of the horizoned breast
The human flesh lighted
                    like a lamp.
All lighted
        corn beetle
                and hill of dust
Hey a hey
        and thanks   grandmother!

Surround of Rainbows

The doorway to my home is made of light
Restore and return the body
                    call it home.
Walk toward me now
Let all tongues ring
Quicken the thighs and breast
            the brain clangs
Strikes the horizon bell
all quickens
all things open in the She Rain.
Growing happily
        We return to our herds
                to our hogans
                        to jingling tassels
                            belling of sheep.
Someone is drumming
                    beating the sky.
Corn reaches up
        She Rain reaches down
Juices spring out of dry thorns
Forgotten bones flesh with forgotten men.
I entered the living water
            It fell upon my starving bones.
Blue corn tied with white lightning
                and the rains come
        upon me too.
Restore us all
The land the man the woman child beast
Insect   all creatures beasts and herbs
Restore us here
Tie us with the blue bean, the great squash

Surround of rainbows
            Listen
The rain comes upon us
            Restore us.

Make the Earth Bright   and Thanks

I am making the sacred smoke
That all the people may behold it.
We are passing with great power
            over the prairie.
The light is upon our people
Making the earth bright
Feathers of sage and cedar
            upon our breasts
Shaking on wrists, ankles,
The tail of the red fox lighting us.
We are crying for a vision.
Behold me that my people may live.
Our people are generous
This is our day.
Your ancestors have all arrived.
The past has arrived
                Behold!
                Listen!
All is established here
We are relatives.
This planet earth
            and all upon it
Turns into view.
This earth is in our hands
Let it fly, bird of earth and light
All that moves will rejoice
Hey a hey a hey!
Approach in a beautiful manner

Approach in your best buckskin
Thanks, all the people are crying
And thanks, grandmother of the center
Of the earth
        Thanks!

DENISE LEVERTOV

The Goddess

She in whose lipservice
I passed my time,
whose name I knew, but not her face,
came upon me where I lay in Lie Castle!

Flung me across the room, and
room after room (hitting the walls, re-
bounding—to the last
sticky wall—wrenching away from it
pulled hair out!)
till I lay
outside the outer walls!

There in cold air
lying still where her hand had thrown me,
I tasted the mud that splattered my lips:
the seeds of a forest were in it,
asleep and growing! I tasted
her power!

The silence was answering my silence,
a forest was pushing itself
out of sleep between my submerged fingers.

I bit on a seed and it spoke on my tongue
of day that shone already among stars
in the water-mirror of low ground,
and a wind rising ruffled the lights:
she passed near me returning from the encounter,
she who plucked me from the close rooms,

without whom nothing
flowers, fruits, sleeps in season,
without whom nothing
speaks in its own tongue, but returns
lie for lie!

The Postcards: A Triptych

The Minoan Snake Goddess is flanked by a Chardin still-life, somber
and tranquil, and by Mohammedan angels
brilliantly clothed and with multicolored wings,
who throng round a fleshcolored horse with a man's face
on whose back rides a white-turbanned being without a face,
merely a white, oval disk, and whose hands too are unformed, or
                                                        hidden
in blue sleeves.
                    Are the angels bringing attributes
  to this unconscious one?
Is he about to be made human?
                              One bends to the floor of heaven in
                                              prayer;
one brings a bowl (of water?) another a tray (of food?); two
point the way, one watches from on high, two and two more
indicate measure, that is, they present
limits that confine the way to a single path;
two debate the outcome, the last
prays not bowed down but looking
level towards the pilgrim.

Stars and the winding
ceintures of the angels surround
the gold cloud or flame before which he rides; heaven itself
is a dark blue.
                    Meanwhile the still-life offers, makes possible,
a glass of water, a wine-bottle made of glass so dark it is
almost black yet not opaque, half full of
perhaps water; and beside these, two courgettes
with rough, yellow-green, almost reptilian skins,
        and a shallow basket
of plums, each almost cleft
with ripeness, the bloom upon them, their skin
darker purple or almost crimson where a hand
touched them, placing them here. Surely
this table, these fruits, these vessels, this water
stand in a cool room, stonefloored, quiet.
And the Goddess?
                    She stands
between the worlds.
                    She is ivory,
her breast bare, her bare arms
braceleted with gold snakes. Their heads
uprear towards her in homage.
Gold borders the tiers of her skirt, a gold hoop
is locked round her waist. She is a few inches high.
And she muses, her lips are pursed,
beneath her crown that must once have been studded with gold
she frowns, she gazes
at and beyond her snakes as if
not goddess but priestess, waiting
an augury.
                    Without thought I have placed these images
over my desk. Under these signs
I am living.

The Dragonfly-Mother

I was setting out from my house
to keep my promise

but the Dragonfly-Mother stopped me.

I was to speak to a multitude
for a good cause, but at home

the Dragonfly-Mother was listening
not to a speech but to the creak of
                    stretching tissue,
tense hum of leaves unfurling.

Who is the Dragonfly-Mother?
What does she do?

She is the one who hovers
on stairways of air,
                    sometimes almost
grazing your cheekbone,
she is the one who darts unforeseeably
into unsuspected dimensions,

who sees in water
her own blue fire zigzag, and lifts
her self in laughter
into the tearful pale sky

that sails blurred clouds in the stream.

                    •

She sat at my round table,
we told one another dreams,
I stayed home breaking my promise.

When she left I slept
three hours, and arose

and wrote. I remember the cold
Waterwoman, in dragonfly dresses

and blue shoes, long ago.
She is the same,

whose children were thin,
left at home when she went out dancing.
She is the Dragonfly-Mother,

that cold
is only the rush of air

swiftness brings.
There is a summer
over the water, over

the river mirrors
where she hovers, a summer
fertile, abundant, where dreams
grow into acts and journeys.

Her children
are swimmers, nymphs and newts, metamorphic.
                              When she tells
her stories she listens; when she listens
she tells you the story you utter.

                    •

When I broke my promise,
and slept, and later

cooked and ate the food she had bought
and left in my kitchen,

I kept a tryst with myself,
a long promise that can be fulfilled
only poem by poem,
broken over and over.

I too,
a creature, grow among reeds,
in mud, in air,
in sunbright cold, in fever
of blue-gold zenith, winds
of passage.

Dragonfly-Mother's
a messenger,
if I don't trust her
I can't keep faith.

There is a summer
in the sleep
of broken promises, fertile dreams,
acts of passage, hovering
journeys over the fathomless waters.

LYNN LONIDIER

Invocation

In Cretan cypress forest clearing   salt-heightened eyelid Priestesses
sway stark-eyed with snakes and tower heads   Skirts swallow wind
Breath of seasight rustles clitoris in anemone harmony

Farmlands smoulder artifacts   Men loosen dirt from conch shells : a
crystal vase : a clay dove : an ivory gaming table   :   the Swinging
Goddess :   Blue Monkeys dug up by doubledouble-edged Man with a
                                                                      Handle

With mighty skirts spread and breasts starting the world   women
embossed in ritual upon gold rings   step in a whirlpool o' poppy pods
Sistrum's   tintinabular   given over to uneartherers notegatherers

Sistrum

A musical
instrument Isis
set in motion in Egypt
to ward off Greed. Enfeebled
in museums a few examples are left
to memory. Round and made of strips
of wood Has a handle Is held aloft. In
side is a hard hollow ball Inside the ball
four harder objects like four dice (air ! earth
fire! water) which when set spinning inside the
ball rotating around the cage hitting rounded
slates of wood create a hyena sound Quickens
hair. No one knows its sound like the bull
roarer rushes air cracking crackling shock
o' snakes in lovely motion O as Hecate's
golden sphere twirled by thong o' leather
shows its sapphire center— hidden past
hidden future (oracular) hidden presence
Created in the shape o' the path o'
the moon Rattle circulates the sky
our ancient sisters used to set
themselves alive We won't pass
imagining its sound Wheels of
a lion-headed woman-driven
chariot drawn by lions
(revive) 'til once the
sistrum
sings
the
sistrum
sings

Reading of the Rattlesnake

Such a dangerous thing
for two women to do;
you sitting there translating
Spanish for me sitting there
—two squeamish women alone-
reading a theory about
how geometric patterns on
rattlesnakes' backs
were the foundation
of Mayan civilization.
You speak of people in Mexico
meting out land by the perfect length
of poisonous snakes; how Aztecs
settled on a bed of snakes,
got rid of the snakes
by eating them.
The book states pre-Columbians
read the stars by rattler designs.
I show you by flashlight
how the city shed its skin.
A Spanish street sign now reads,
"A Girls' Gang."
You tell me La Raza teenage girls
get together and design their own
low cars with their own
vibrant pipes, fanfare rainbow hoods,
fur-lined cave interiors.
And I tell you about the fifth-grade
girl matriarchy among Chicano-Latino
children where I work. O it's
a dangerous world slowly
being infiltrated by diamonds,
curving rectangles on the
rattlesnake's back. (La Curva
is making major decisions!)
I listen to your beaded tales
unwind a string o' jeweled

heart-truths.
The shape of a bead of a rattle
is that of a heart; each one
proportionately larger in size,
like a pyramid,
like a city,
like sin.
Sin turns into quiet pets
on our laps. Loving words,
two women on a couch unflinchingly
touch pages picturing snakes.

Mediterranean Snake Admitter

To admit the beauty of a snake,
give it a room of its own.

Place a statue of a woman holding lightning-bolts
on a ledge in the room.

Put a low table made of red clay in the room,
table balanced on three legs.

Fashion the top of the snake table with four
evenly-spaced, intersecting troughs, to form a cross.

At the intersecting point of the two sides of the cross,
hollow a hole for the feeding dish of the snakes to fit.

Place the snakes' food in shallow terracotta bowls.
Leave out barley kernels, honey cakes, milk,

grub worms and pieces of cheese.
Make a hollow clay pipe with holes for the snakes to crawl

up and out onto ledges where each can rest or eat or bask.
Call the pipe, "snake tube."

Line temple floors and hall archways
with 〰〰〰〰 the notched plume ornament.

Design the flounced skirt of the chryselephantine goddess
or the borders of portable hearths,

or The Tomb of the Tripod Hearth
with the ornament of the notched plume.

Paint the wave and dot pattern arterial red
and the background a deep tawny wheat white.

Recognize the rows of waves with intermittent dots
you're creating is not a notched plume

but the design on the adder snake's back.
Know the adder also as the "cat snake,"

but it solely eats lizards and mice.
Learn the fangs of the sacred adder are too far back

in its mouth to seize the limb of a human
and deliver a deadly sting.

Research that the adder is no longer found on Crete
and the adder was once endemic to Crete.

Regard the adder as the Mother of the Sphinx.
Observe adder marks on wings of sphinxes and griffins.

Be assured the way priestesses held their snakes,
they loved them.

See the snake gazing up at Her fondly?
Feel that if a snake appears, it is a long lost

intimate ancestor, and you and your garden are
entranced with the new skin of its entrance.

The Swinging Goddess—
Sally Ride; First American Woman Astronaut

                    the the
                the swinging swinging the
            the swinging headless headless swinging the
        the swinging headless goddess goddess headless singing the
    swinging headless goddess headless swinging says   her head is missing

Without her head archeologists surmise the swinging goddess the swinging
goddess   may be nothing but a child's toy child's toy   How could she
be a goddess   without a crown how could she have a crown without a head
The swinging goddess is using her brain to swing high without a head
without a crown

Archeologists with heads on acknowledge   pillars on either side of
the swinging goddess's swing   each supports a dove   and   such signs
indicate Presence of the Goddess Aloft

As the figure swings   the wind sings a little song out of her missing
mouth
            O have you swung lately
                you
            have you have
                you sung lately
                    in the skyday sun a woman's in the sky today,
                                sky today, sky today,
                                a woman went up in the sky today,
                                easy Evie over and out.
                                She went yes! out of the house
                                and u-huh! above the garden wall,
                                like a necktie on a lady,
                                straight up, yep! Eve slipped
                                through bible night trying to
                                net her like a housewife in the sky.
                                She's the wide-eyed newborn
                    floating about the starry clime of her origin—
                    Libyan air returned to forest.

                    Get yourself a man, Man,
                        another man, yep! a man for a man, Yes!
As he retracts his rib, centuries-slow Adam
    births compassion beyond what he's fucked lately, u-huh!
                            The weightless swinging goddess
                            steered him off his perch
        and out under the moon   to touch
            his finger   to another   man   and Eve   without him
lives to find female
                flying
                    companions   New earthfoundlings explore awe

Most expectant happy landing says the swinging goddess swinging the
swinging goddess swinging the swinging headless swinging the the
swinging headless goddess headless swinging the the swinging headless
goddess says goddess headless swinging lately swung lately sung sings
on an ocher island   in an aqua ocean

AUDRE LORDE

~~~~~~

The Winds of Orisha

I

This land will not always be foreign.
How many of its women ache to bear their stories
robust and screaming like the earth erupting grain
or thrash in padded chains mute as bottles
hands fluttering traces of resistance
on the backs of once lovers
half the truth
knocking in the brain like an angry steampipe
how many
long to work or split open
so bodies venting into silence
can plan the next move?

Tiresias took 5OO years they say to progress into woman
growing smaller and darker and more powerful
until nut-like, she went to sleep in a bottle
Tiresias took 5OO years to grow into woman
so do not despair of your sons.

II

Impatient legends speak through my flesh
changing this earth's formation
spreading

I will become myself
an incantation
dark raucous many-shaped characters
leaping back and forth across bland pages
and Mother Yemanja raises her breasts to begin my labor
near water
the beautiful Oshun and I lie down together
in the heat of her body truth my voice comes stronger
Shango will be my brother roaring out of the sea
earth shakes our darkness swelling into each other
warning winds will announce us living
as Oya, Oya my sister my daughter
destroys the crust of the tidy beaches
and Eshu's black laughter turns up the neat sleeping sand.

III

The heart of this country's tradition is its wheat men
dying for money
dying for water for markets for power
over all people's children
they sit in their chains on their dry earth
before nightfall
telling tales as they wait for their time
of completion
hoping the young ones can hear them
earth-shaking fears wreathe their blank weary faces
most of them have spent their lives and their wives
in labor
most of them have never seen beaches
but as Oya my sister moves out of the mouths
of their sons and daughters against them
I will swell up from the pages of their daily heralds
leaping out of the almanacs
instead of an answer to their search for rain they will read me
the dark cloud
meaning something entire
and different.

When the winds of Orisha blow
even the roots of grass
quicken.

October

Spirits
of the abnormally born
live on in water
of the heroically dead
in the entrails of snake.
Now I span my days like a wild bridge
swaying in place
caught between poems like a vise
I am finishing my piece of this bargain
and how shall I return?

Seboulisa, mother of power
keeper of birds
fat and beautiful
give me the strength of your eyes
to remember
what I have learned
help me to attend with passion
these tasks at my hand for doing.

Carry my heart to some shore
that my feet will not shatter
do not let me pass away
before I have a name

for this tree
under which I am lying.
Do not let me die
still
needing to be stranger.

Call

Holy ghost woman
stolen out of your name
Rainbow Serpent
whose faces have been forgotten
Mother loosen my tongue or adorn me
with a lighter burden
Aido Hwedo is coming.

On worn kitchen stools and tables
we are piecing our weapons together
scraps of different histories
do not let us shatter
any altar
she who scrubs the capitol toilets, listening
is our sister's youngest daughter
gnarled Harriet's anointed
you have not been without honor
even the young guerrilla has chosen
yells as she fires into the thicket
Aido Hwedo is coming.

I have written your names on my cheekbone
dreamed your eyes   flesh my epiphany
most ancient goddesses   hear me
enter
I have not forgotten your worship
nor my sisters
nor the sons of my daughters
my children watch for your print
in their labors
and they say Aido Hwedo is coming.

I am a Black woman   turning
mouthing your name as a password
through seductions   self-slaughter
and I believe in the holy ghost
mother

in your flames beyond our vision
blown light through the fingers of women
enduring   warring
sometimes outside your name
we do not choose all our rituals
Thandi Modise   winged girl of Soweto
brought fire back home in the snout of a mortar
and passes the word from her prison cell whispering
Aido Hwedo is coming.

Rainbow Serpent who must not go
unspoken
I have offered up the safety of separations
sung the spirals of power
and what fills the spaces
before power unfolds or flounders
in desirable nonessentials
I am a Black woman   stripped down
and praying
my whole life has been an altar
worth its ending
and I say Aido Hwedo is coming.

I may be a weed in the garden
of women I have loved
who are still
trapped in their season
but even they shriek
as they rip burning gold from their skins
Aido Hwedo is coming.

We are learning by heart
what has never been taught
you are my given   fire-tongued
Oya   Seboulisa   Mawu   Afrekete
and now we are mourning our sisters
lost to the false hush of sorrow
to hardness and hatchets and childbirth
and we are shouting

Rosa Parks and Fannie Lou Hamer
Assata Shakur and Yaa Asantewa
my mother and Winnie Mandela are singing
in my throat
the holy ghosts' linguist
one iron silence broken
Aido Hwedo is calling
calling
your daughters are named
and conceiving
Mother   loosen my tongue
or adorn me
with a lighter burden
Aido Hwedo is coming.

Aido Hwedo is coming.

Aido Hwedo is coming.

Aido Hwedo: The Rainbow Serpent; also a representation of all ancient divinities who must
be worshiped but whose names and faces have been lost in time.

MARY MACKEY

~~~~~~

The Woman in the Moon

my great-grandmother
married at sixteen
a blue-eyed Irish woodworker
who promised to build her
a life out of apple wood
and cherry
instead he gave her
thirteen children
drank up the rent
and died of blood poisoning
while building a carriage
shaped like a shoe

for forty years
she lived alone
dressed in black
like a retired witch
in a house full of chests
and chairs and wood clocks
waiting for him
to come home again

when she was eighty

and I was four
we met
her skin was so thin
by then that you could
see her veins like grain
she kept her teeth
in a glass of water
and her heart in a rosewood
box by the door

there is a woman
in the moon
my great-grandmother told me
who carries a bundle of sticks
on her back

each month she swells
each month she declines
like many women
she has married a burden
and must bear it forever
across the sky

life bends us, she told me
my own life was scrapwood
my own life was sorrow
as thick as a board

tell all your daughters
to build something better
burn kindling
not carry
keep one eye on the sky.

On the Dark Side of the Moon

on the dark side of the moon
a golden egg lay in a crater
shaped like the pause
between two breaths
beat like a heart
a hummingbird hidden
in the palm of my hand

I swallowed it whole
felt it roll inside me
unsteady as a half loaded ship
riding an invisible tide

on the seventh wave the egg
penetrated my womb
and I became pregnant with space
immaculate and alien
the whites of my eyes gold
my lips my hands gold
foil skin beaten out across my cheeks
gold swelling from my hips
I was the expanding universe
I gave birth to marvelous creatures

one spoke in colors instead of words
another was covered with small dry twigs
the third lay storms to rest
the fourth made orchards grow
where bones had been

the fifth was a blue messiah
she fed the world at her breast
she trimmed the dead leaves from plants
with the cutting edge of her desire
her fingers were like a field of green wheat
she drove souls before her like warm rain

the sixth came to destroy all impediments
he levelled the hills and burnished
the earth to a ball
there was a glass in my bread
I gave birth to the seventh while lying
on a mirror

the egg inside me cracked
I rose and created a new creation
I invented animals
I organized the clouds
I swung the moon around
in a pause between two breaths

this is a true story
I know
I dreamed it.

Betony

by the time
we came across the gap
through the Cumberlands
it was late spring
and I was driving the wagon alone
my husband was buried
under a buckeye tree
five days back
two of the children
had milk fever
and the third lay
sick at my breast

it was a violent
blue-green Kentucky spring

mushrooms raised their humps
over every log
and the waters were roiled
with strange fish

the first year we ate
acorns and nearly starved

you need a husband
the neighbors said

the second year
the cabin burned
and I covered my children
with leaves
and nested down with them
like a squirrel

you can't live without a man
my neighbors told me

the third year
we ate our own corn
at our own table
the forest around us was blessed
we killed nothing
the earth opened up to our seeds
the sun and the rain
came in perfect order
and the squashes in the garden
swelled like pregnant women

I took coltsfoot and barberry
and conceived a fourth child
she was born with a tiny ring
of blood around her wrist
and her eyes were as soft
as new bark
when she walked

wildflowers grew in her footprints
her bones were fine and hollow
she flew over her sisters
like a jackdaw

I called her Betony
and the neighbors said
I was mad

she will grow sweet to the taste
I told them
she will cure all wounds
she will be Betony
the spiked plant
the wood mint
the woman alone
who sanctifies.

Cytherea

Quivering fins
ridged like rakes
a sliding, gill-chambered tongue—
the inside of her mouth
is yellow and blue
barracuda silver
sweet as red mullet
stripped with black and green
with peacock flounder teeth
pink and sharp and quick

Cytherea is angry
that we have poisoned her oceans
at night she climbs the waves
straddles the white foam

and calls to her whales
"are you catfood yet?"
she howls
"have the Japanese made you all
into lipstick and soup?"

She is unforgiving
and methodical
when a dolphin gets tangled
in a tuna net
she grieves
when a single cell of green algae dies
she knows it

She has picked the brains
of all the philosophers who ever drowned
looking for the causes of human folly
she has mastered the concept of original sin
and thinks there may be something to it
she is acquainted with the theory of eternal forms
that holds that if the oceans of earth die
the idea of oceans will persist unchanged
in some godly sphere of boredom and perfection
but the only oceans Cytherea cares about
are these
bitter and dirty
salty and dying
these small mortal oceans
it makes her weep to see them

the rusting barrels of nuclear waste
drive Cytherea to distraction
she plots revenge
with the cunning of a shark—she
who was so peaceful
that the Phoenician sailors
wrote odes to her patience
calling her dove soft
smoother than their wives

purple skinned and lovely
as the harbor of Tyre
when the shellfish blossom
oh lovely sea goddess
they wrote,
we move across your belly
like bridegrooms
singing your praises

Now she sits in a dark cave
consorting with morays
sipping poison drinks
concocted from the venom
of Australian stone fish
counting the tankers
that rumble overhead
breathing the oil-fouled water
assimilating the toxins
through her seaweed soft skin
she is not pleased
she is not amused

Cytherea is planning something
down there
something she tells only
to the spiny batfish
and the sea dragons
perhaps she has decided
to call back the oxygen
and leave us gasping
perhaps she has decided
to melt her ice caps
rise and take back all the cities
that ever emptied sewage
down her throat
perhaps she has decided to show us
a mercy we don't deserve—
but don't count on it

Cytherea
the flowers we throw to you
come back oil-soaked
and dying
We stand on your beaches
calling you up
but you no longer appear
at our feet you scatter
pieces of styrofoam cups
tin cans, beer bottles, hunks of insulation,
stinking fish and dead birds
and sometimes a jelly fish
pulsing and dying
like a punctured soap bubble
like a human heart
gone bad.

ROBIN MORGAN

~~~~~~

The Two Gretels

The two Gretels were exploring the forest.
Hansel was home,
sending up flares.

Sometimes one Gretel got afraid.
She said to the other Gretel,
"I think I'm afraid."
"Of course we are," Gretel replied.

Sometimes the other Gretel whispered,
with a shiver,
"You think we should turn back?"
To which her sister Gretel answered,
"We can't. We forgot the breadcrumbs."

So, they went forward
because
they simply couldn't imagine the way back.

And eventually, they found the Gingerbread House,
and the Witch, who was really, they discovered,
the Great Good Mother Goddess,
and they all lived happily ever after.

The Moral of this story is:

Those who would have the whole loaf,
let alone the House,
had better throw away their breadcrumbs.

A Ceremony

A clearing in a grove of oak,
night sounds, and water rushing
along a canyon river.
Two candles moved through the trees,
two women. The flames curved in the summer wind
like liquid leaning into gravity.

The light encircled us,
the moonrays palpable and warm.
Our pilgrimage along the dried stream-bed
completed, we stood before three giant Cacti:
virgin, mother, crone—
round as massive cabbage roses
in a sacred cluster.

The roseate cactus,
seal of all my madness,
whose circle of white-tipped spines
I once had seen reach for me, stretch
for the impaling of my drawn face.

Now you said
you had never seen my lips
wear such a smile before.
Nor had I ever heard your voice like this:
sweet, high, and clear as my child's singing.
We lit the incense we had brought with us

and watched its smoke trace our calligraphy
upon a slate of air.

There is almost no one who would understand
what we were doing, and not doing, there.
There were no categories for that space.
It was simply that we had been spoken of by others
for so long, and now we spoke ourselves,
uttering a silver ring, a silver pentacle,
a cup of wine spilled carefully.
Some would have said we were not even lovers.

Look, we have left the grove.
We will grow old, and older.
One of us will die, and then the other.
The earth itself will be impaled
on sunspokes. It doesn't matter.
We have been imprinted on the protons
of energy herself,

and so stand in another atmosphere,
where an undiscovered star we will never live to see
casts shadows on a grove of succulents we cannot yet imagine.
There our interchangeable features still vibrate and blur,
each smile half of one circle,
each utterance spiraling like light
upward in shudders along the spine
as if the moon and you and I were slivers
of one mirror, gazing on herself at last.

The Self (*from* The Network of the Imaginary Mother)

Each unblinking eyelet linked now
to another in the shuttles of the loom.
"Thin rainbow-colored nets, like cobwebs,
all over my skin."
I affirm
all
of my transformations:

>An autumnal mother, treading the way of life
>>past all her trials, yearns toward her Albion,
>>leprous-white as waterlilies.
>Returning to herself, a daughter who reflects
>>a different dawn emerges, reckless as the weeds
>>that array her vernal equinox.
>The chosen man, given over at last, discards his shroud
>>for love's reweaving, initiate to what
>>the ecstatic Widow male has always known, the secret
>>of the young king at winter solstice—
>And so is born again, shameless, laughing,
>>to reach past fear, through reverence, to touch
>>what it is like, this being alive.

These are my people.

They are of my willing, of my own making.
I have invented them no less than I create myself,
thought imagining shape, uttering existence.
To understand this universe I fabricate
—my cosmic joke, embodied plot—
I am become the Spinner, giving out of myself
myself the Egg,
taking into myself
myself the Prey.

Witch-queen, sorceress,
I must live within this body, my final home—
here to decode each runic fingerprint,
to trust the assurance of each hair's whitening,

to recognize the clue left by each stretch-mark.
My taste is salty, my smell ammonial.
My knuckles can crack like willow-bark
and hairblades cover my hide
stubborn as fine grass.
My nails are crisp as relics
and every crevice—armpits, crotch,
toe-valleys, ears, mouth, nostrils, eyes—exudes
mucous or sweat for iridescence.
Oh let me learn that I am beautiful to me,
innocent as the spider—
beyond judgment, disgust, beyond perfection—
reconciled with her tufted claw,
with the matted topaz of my labia.
Let me sit at the center of myself
and see with all my eyes,
speak with both my mouths,
feel with all my setae,
know my own sharp pleasure,
learning at last and blessedly and utterly:
The life comes first. There is no spirit without the form.

Drawn from the first by what I would become,
I did not know how simple this secret could be.
The carapace is split,
the shed skin lies upon the ground.
I must devour the exoskeleton of my old shapes,
wasting no part, free only then
to radiate whatever I conceive,
to exclaim the strongest natural fiber known
into such art, such architecture
as can house a world made sacred by my building.
Sheet method, funnel, and orb,
each thread of the well-named Ariadna
unreels its lesson:

The Triangle web, three-faced as my aspects;
the filmy Dome web, a model firmament;
the domesticity of the Bowl-and-Doily web;

the droll zig-zag of the Filistata;
the Hammock pattern's indolence;
the Coras web, with healing power for welts and fever;
the Trapdoor web, shield of the White Lady from the desert;
the Arabesca, the Dictyna;
the vaporous Platform web;
the Umbrella's unfolding tension;
the esoteric Pyramid design;
the Purse web, tubed and tightly wattled;
the Bubble web, patience iterated underwater,
a crystal castle of air.

Here is discipline, imagination, variation.
Here are your paragons, my avatars.

I am learning.
The cord is wrapped around my throat.
I am learning.
The passageway is cramped and blind
I am learning
though Kali dances through it, past
where Demeter still seeks Persephone,
where Isis searches for the fragments of Osiris,
where I wade upstream through a living current
which seizes me and drowns me into life,
pumping, pumping, as from a giant heart
whose roar I have called Mother in my dreams.

> *What do you remember?*
> *What is it that you long for still?*

Oh let me hear you hear
me speak oh
speak to
me oh let me

> *Repeat the syllables*
> *each cell has unforgotten:*
> *There was the Word before their word.*

The Silence came.
The Name was changed.

What have they done to themselves?

What have they dared,
sucking at man's wounds for wine,
celebrating his flesh as food?
Whose thirst has been slaked by his vampire liquor,
whose hunger answered by his ghostly bread?

Who have they dared to hang on that spine instead
and then deny, across millennia?
Whose is the only body which incarnates creation
everlasting?

As it was in the beginning,
I say:
Here is your sacrament—

Take. Eat. This is my body,
this real milk, thin, sweet, bluish,
which I give for the life of the world.
Like sap to spring it rises
even before the first faint cry is heard,
an honest nourishment
alone able to sustain you.

I say:
Here is your eternal testament—

This cup, this chalice, this primordial cauldron
of real menstrual blood
the color of clay warm with promise,
rhythmic, cyclical, fit for lining the uterus
and shed for many,
for the remission of living.

Here is your bread of life.
Here is the blood by which you live in me.

The World Disc, The Great Round,
The Wheel of Transformation.
Two solstices, summer and winter.
Two equinoxes, spring and fall.
One day to stand outside the year, unutterable.
Thirteen-fold is my lunar calendar,
Five-fold my mysteries, my kiss,
Three-fold my face.

> And this is the secret, once unquestioned,
> sought in the oldest trances of us all:
> the large male children forced into exile
> from their pelvic cradle, wailing, refusing to leave;
> the grown female children, knotting together the skein
> of generations, each loop in the coil a way back
> to that heart of memory we cannot escape,
> yet long for still.

No more need you dream this, my children,
in remembrance of me.
There is a place beyond your struggle
where I will exist us.
It will exist, see, I am creating it now.
I have said so.

> Blessed be my brain
>   that I may conceive of my own power.
> Blessed be my breast
>   that I may give sustenance to those I love.
> Blessed be my womb
>   that I may create what I choose to create.
> Blessed be my knees
>   that I may bend so as not to break.
> Blessed be my feet
>   that I may walk in the path of my highest will.

Now is the seal of my vision
set upon my flesh.

You call me by a thousand names, uttering yourselves.

      Earthquake I answer you, flood and volcano flow—
          the Warning.
          This to remind you that I am the Old One
          who holds the Key, the Crone to whom all things return.

      Lotus I answer you, lily, corn-poppy, centripetal rose—
          the Choice.
          This to remind you that I am the Mother
          who unravels from herself the net sustaining you.

      Moon I answer you, my gibbous eye, the regenerating carapace,
          the Milky Way—
          the Possibility.
          This to remind you that I am the Virgin
          born only now, new, capable of all invention.

I have been with you from the beginning,
utterly simple.
I will be with you when you die,
say what you will.
We shall never be finished.
This is possible,
a small gift, hush.

There is nothing I have not been,
and I am come into my power.

There is nothing I cannot be.

MARGE PIERCY

The Window of the Woman Burning

Woman dancing with hair
on fire, woman writhing in the
cone of orange snakes, flowering
into crackling lithe vines:
Woman
you are not the bound witch
at the stake, whose broiled alive
agonized screams
thrust from charred flesh
darkened Europe in the nine millions.
Woman
you are not the madonna impaled
whose sacrifice of self leaves her
empty and mad as wind,
or whore crucified
studded with nails.

Woman
you are the demon of a fountain of energy
rushing up from the coal hard
memories in the ancient spine,
flickering lights from the furnace in the solar
plexus, lush scents from the reptilian brain,

river that winds up the hypothalamus
with its fibroids of pleasure and pain
twisted and braided like rope,
firing the lanterns of the forebrain
till they glow blood red.

You are the fire sprite
that charges leaping thighs,
that whips the supple back on its arc
as deer leap through the ankles:
dance of a woman strong
in beauty that crouches
inside like a cougar in the belly
not in the eyes of others measuring.

You are the icon of woman sexual
in herself like a great forest tree
in flower, liriodendron bearing sweet tulips,
cups of joy and drunkenness.
You drink strength from your dark fierce roots
and you hang at the sun's own fiery breast
and with the green cities of your boughs
you shelter and celebrate
woman, with the cauldrons of your energies
burning red, burning green.

Athena in the Front Lines

Only accidents preserve.
Athena Promachos, warrior goddess thirty feet tall,
no longer exists. Phidias
made her between wars in ruins
of a fort that had not kept the enemy out.
Making is an attack too, on bronze, on air, on time.
Sailors out on the Argo-Saronic

of gull and dolphin and bone-dry island
could see the sunlight creaking on her helmet.
A thousand years she stood over fire and mud,
then hauled as booty to Constantinople,
where the Crusaders, bouncy legionnaires
on the town, melted her down for coins.

These words are pebbles
sucked from mouth to mouth since Chaucer.
I don't believe the Etruscans or the Mayans
lacked poets, only victories.
Manuscripts under glass, women's quilts packed away
lie in the attics of museums sealed from the streets
where the tactical police are clubbing the welfare mothers.
There are no cameras, so it is not real.

Wring the stones of the hillside
for the lost plays of Sophocles they heard.
Art is nonaccident. Like love, it is
a willed tension up through the mind
balancing thrust and inertia, energy
stored in a bulb. Then the golden
trumpet of the narcissus pokes up
willfully into the sun, focusing the world.

The epigraphs stabbed the Song of Songs
through the smoking heart (The Church
Prepares for Her Bridegroom). The seven hundred thousand
four hundred fifty second tourist stared
the Venus de Milo into a brassiere ad.
Generations of women wrote poems and hid
them in drawers, because an able
woman is a bad woman. They expired
leaking radioactivity among pastel underwear.

A woman scribbling for no one doodles,
dabbles in madness, dribbles shame.
Art requires a plaza in the mind, a space
lit by the sun of regard. That tension

between maker and audience, that feedback,
that force field of interest, sustains
an I less guilty than Ego, who can utter
the truths of vision and nightmare,
the truths that spill like raw egg from the
cracking of body on body, the thousand
soft and slimy names of death, the songs
of the blind fish that swim
the caverns of bone, the songs
of the hawks who soar and stoop grappling
and screaming through the crystalline
skies of the forehead.

Though the cod stifle in the seas, though
the rivers thicken to shit, still
writing implies faith in someone listening,
different in content but not in need
from the child who cries in the night.

Making is an attack on dying, on chaos.
on blind inertia, on the second law
of thermodynamics, on indifference, on cold,
on contempt, on the silence
that does not follow the chord resolved,
the sentence spoken, but the something
that cannot be said. Perhaps there are no
words yet, perhaps the words bend the thought
back on itself, perhaps the words can be said
but cannot yet be heard, and so
the saying arches through the air and crumbles.

Making is an act, but survival
is luck, caught in history
like a moth trapped in the subway.
There is nothing to do but make well,
finish, and let go. Words
live, words die
in the mouths of everybody.

The Sabbath of Mutual Respect

In the natural year come two thanksgivings,
the harvest of summer and the harvest of fall,
two times when we eat and drink and remember our dead
under the golden basin of the moon of plenty.

Abundance, Habondia, food for the winter,
too much now and survival later. After
the plant bears, it dies into seed.
The blowing grasses nourish us, wheat
and corn and rye, millet and rice, oat
and barley and buckwheat, all the serviceable
grasses of the pasture that the cow grazes,
the lamb, the horse, the goat; the grasses
that quicken into meat and cheese and milk,
the humble necessary mute vegetable bees,
the armies of the grasses waving their
golden banners of ripe seed.
                       The sensual
round fruit that gleams with the sun
stored in its sweetness.
                       The succulent
ephemera of the summer garden, bloodwarm
tomatoes, tender small squash, crisp
beans, the milky corn, the red peppers
exploding like cherry bombs in the mouth.

We praise abundance by eating of it,
reveling in choice on a table set with roses
and lilies and phlox, zucchini and lettuce
and eggplant before the long winter
of root crops.
                 Fertility and choice:
every row dug in spring means weeks
of labor. Plant too much and the seedlings
choke in weeds as the warm rain soaks them.
The goddess of abundance Habondia is also
the spirit of labor and choice.

                    In another
life, dear sister, I too would bear six fat
children. In another life, my sister, I too
would love another woman and raise one child
together as if that pushed from both our wombs.
In another life, sister, I too would dwell
solitary and splendid as a lighthouse on the rocks
or be born to mate for life like the faithful goose.
Praise all our choices. Praise any woman
who chooses, and make safe her choice.

Habondia, Artemis, Cybele, Demeter, Ishtar,
Aphrodite, Au Set, Hecate, Themis, Lilith,
Thea, Gaia, Bridgit, The Great Grandmother of Us
All, Yemanja, Cerridwen, Freya, Corn Maiden,
Mawu, Amaterasu, Maires, Nut, Spider-Woman,
Neith, Au Zit, Hathor, Inanna, Shin Moo,
Diti, Arinna, Anath, Tiamat, Astoreth:
the names flesh out our histories, our choices,
our passions and what we will never embody
but pass by with respect. When I consecrate
my body in the temple of our history,
when I pledge myself to remain empty
and clear for the voices coming through
I do not choose for you or lessen your choice.

Habondia, the real abundance, is the power
to say yes and to say no, to open
and to close, to take or to leave
and not to be taken by force or law
or fear or poverty or hunger.
To bear children or not to bear by choice
is holy. To bear children unwanted
is to be used like a public sewer.
To be sterilized unchosen is to have
your heart cut out. To love women
is holy and holy is the free love of men
and precious to live taking whichever comes
and precious to live unmated as a peachtree.

Praise the lives you did not choose.
They will heal you, tell your story, fight
for you. You eat the bread of their labor.
You drink the wine of their joy. I tell you
after I went under the surgeon's knife
for the laparoscopy I felt like a trumpet
an Amazon was blowing sonorous charges on.
Then my womb learned to open on the full
moon without pain and my pleasure deepened
till my body shuddered like troubled water.
When my friend gave birth I held her in joy
as the child's head thrust from her vagina
like the sun rising at dawn wet and red.

Praise our choices, sisters, for each doorway
open to us was taken by squads of fighting
women who paid years of trouble and struggle,
who paid their wombs, their sleep, their lives
that we might walk through these gates upright.
Doorways are sacred to women for we
are the doorways of life and we must choose
what comes in and what goes out. Freedom
is our real abundance.

The Longest Night

The longest night is long drawn
as a freight blocking a grade crossing
in a prairie town when I am trying
to reach Kansas City to sleep and one
boxcar clatters after the other, after
and after in faded paint proclaiming
as they trundle through the headlights
names of 19th-century fortunes, scandals,
labor wars. Stalled between factory

and cemetery I lean on the cold wheel.
The factory is still, the machines
turned off; the cemetery looks boring
and factual as a parking lot. Too cold
for the dead to stir, tonight even
my own feel fragile as brown bags
carted to the dump. Ash stains the air.
wheels of the freight clack by. Snow
hisses on the windshield of the rented car.
Always a storm at the winter solstice.

New moon, no moon, old moon dying,
moon that gives no light, stub
of a candle, dark lantern, face
without features, the zone of zero:
I feel the blood starting. Monthly
my womb opens on the full moon but
my body is off its rhythms. I am
jangled and raw. I do not celebrate
this blood seeping as from a wound.
I feel my weakness summoning me
like a bed of soft grey ashes
I might crawl into.

Here in the pit of the year scars overlap
scabs, the craters of the moon, stone
breaking stone. In the rearview mirror
my black hair fades into the night,
my cheeks look skeletal, my dark eyes,
holes a rat might hide in. I sense
death lurking up the road like a feral
dog abroad in the swirling snow.

Defeat, defeat, defeat, tedious
as modern headstones, regular as dentures.
My blood tastes salty as tears and rusty
as an old nail. Yet as I kick the car
over the icy tracks toward nowhere
I want to be, I am grinning. Lady, it's been

worse before, bad as the moon burning,
bad as the moon's horn goring my side,
that to give up now is a joke told
by the FBI minding the tap or the binoculars
staking me out on such a bitter night
when the blood slows and begins to freeze.
I grew up among these smoke-pitted houses
choking over the railroad between the factory
shuddering and the cemetery for the urban
poor, and I got out. They say that's
what you ask for. And how much more
I ask. To get everybody out.

Hecate, lady of the crossroads, vampires
of despair you loose and the twittering
bats of sleepless fear. The three-headed
dog barking in the snow obeys you.
Tonight I honor you, lady of last things.
Without you to goad me I would lie
late in the warm bed of the flesh.
The blood I coughed from my lungs that year
you stood at the foot of my bed was sour,
acrid, the taste of promises broken
and since then I have run twice as fast.
Your teeth are in me, like tiny headstones.
This moon is the void around which the serpent
with its tail in its mouth curls.
Where there is no color, no light,
no sound, what is ? The dark of the mind.
In terror begins vision. In silence
I learn my song, here at the stone
nipple, the black moon bleeding,
the egg anonymous as water,
the night that goes on and on,
a tunnel through the earth.

O!

Oh, the golden bauble of your rising
wet from the waves rippling,
radiating like orgasm, round
as a singing mouth at full stretch,
round as the vagina when it takes,
round as a full belly, round
as a baby's head, you come to us
riding over the white manes
of the waves, walking on their backs
like a circus rider. Hoop
of cool fire, goose egg,
silver mirror in which we see
ourselves dimly but truly reflected,
our blood is salty water
you tug at, drawing us.
Red onion, I peel you layer
by layer and weep. The nights
carve you and then you swell
again, lady of the wild animals
whose homes are paved and poisoned,
lady of the furry mammals at teat
and the shimmering fish whose sides
echo you, of those who hunt for roots
and berries, hunt for the island
in the sea where love rules and women
are free to wax and wane and wander
in the sweet strict seasons
of our desires and needs.

Let Us Gather at the River

I am the woman who sits by the river
river of tears
river of sewage
river of rainbows.
I sit by the river and count the corpses
floating by from the war upstream.
I sit by the river and watch the water
dwindle and the banks poke out like sore gums.
I watch the water change from green to shit brown.
I sit by the river and fish for your soul.
I want to lick it clean.
I want to turn it into a butterfly
that will weave drunkenly from orchid to rose.
I want to turn it into a pumpkin.
I want it to turn itself into a human being.

Oh, close your eyes tight and push hard
and evolve, altogether now. We can
do it if we try. Concentrate
and hold hands and push.
You can take your world back
if you want to. It's an araucana
egg, all blue and green
swaddled in filmy clouds.
Don't let them cook and gobble it,
azure and jungle green egg laid
by the extinct phoenix of the universe.

Send me your worn hacks of tired themes,
your dying horses of liberation,
your poor bony mules of freedom now.
I am the woman sitting by the river.
I mend old rebellions and patch them new.

Now the river turns from shit brown to bubbling blood
as an arm dressed in a uniform
floats by like an idling log.

Up too high to see, bombers big as bowling alleys
streak over and the automated battlefield
lights up like a Star Wars pinball machine.

I am the old woman sitting by the river scolding corpses.
I want to stare into the river and see the bottom
glinting like clean hair.
I want to outlive my usefulness
and sing water songs, songs
in praise of the green brown river
flowing clean through the blue green world.

I Saw Her Dancing

1

Because I saw her change
Because I saw her
                    change
Cuba in the simmering summer of sixty-eight
when the walls of the ghettoed world seemed to be melting
from the heat of our bodies and our blazing minds
into wax dripping down a wine bottle
and the sun itself was the bright candle.

Santos, santaría
Drum speaking to drum
each a heart pounding each a womb throbbing
hands caressing, teasing, spanking, kneading the stretched
     skin.

An old woman was dancing to the drums, in faded cotton skirts
scrawny chicken neck, loose shuddering arms
washerwoman toeing and swirling to the rhythms
when Yemanja came to ride her.

My knees jellied. My eyes burned of smoke.
Then I was turning in place, a top
whirled by a string,
for her face sparkled like a waterfall in sunlight
for her skin was smooth as still water
that plays mirror to the moon's leaning face
for her arms were lithe and snapping snakes
for she swayed tall as a coconut palm
her hips rolled to the waves calling them home
and teasing them out again
        and she changed
        and she changed
        and she changed
and seeing I was shaken like water troubled to the bottom
stones the water punishes and polishes bright.

Then it was again an old woman
flabby and limp and washed out like old cotton shirts
pounded on the rocks and bleached in the sun
too many times and hard years.

2

Because all poets know how the god
seizes you by the nape and shakes till your bones
vibrate all their tuning forks on key
taking you from behind like a great tomcat
mounting you with teeth gripped in your skin
pulling tight, tight as a drum.

Because all artists know the self
is a bag of roaring winds northeast, south, west
coiling for a curious fool to loose them,
and all artists are fools who push on and in
servants of chaos and of order in each season
as Persephone labored to please death and fertility
finding in herself both seed and skull
the flower that opens at each end of life.

Because all women know being used
by what wants to come into the world, by what scratches
and claws and gouges its way toward light,
and then starts screaming its lungs sore,
needing infinite labor just to keep in the air.

                              3
I a Jew saw Yemanja and worshiped
as I have met other goddesses
in dark and shining places.

It is all many as fingers and toes and the hair of your head
and it is all one.
It is all one as an egg, as a seed, as stone, as a fire
and it is all many.

I know I know I know   I am known
in silence liquid and dark as oil
still locked in rock, in the hot peristaltic bowels of earth.

Yanking my hair hard till my eyes tear,
she touches the nape there
breathing out her fiery dragon's breath
and I am changed.

We are lit up and then the light fades out.
I stand in the field pelted with the rain
and wait for the forked gift to electrify me.

Nothing living moves in straight lines
but in arcs, in epicycles, in spirals, in gyres.
Nothing living grows in cubes or cones or rhomboids
but we take a little here and give a little here
and we change
and the wind blows right through us and knocks the apples
from the tree and hangs a red kite suddenly there
and a fox comes to bite the apples curiously
and we change
or die

and then change.
It is many as drops
it is one as rain
and we are in it, in it, of it.
We eat it and it eats us
and fullness is never and now.

The Ram's Horn Sounding, Part III

A woman and a Jew, sometimes more
of a contradiction than I can sweat out,
yet finally the intersection that is both
collision and fusion, stone and seed.

Like any poet I wrestle the holy name
and know there is no wording finally
can map, constrain or summon that fierce
voice whose long wind lifts my hair

chills my skin and fills my lungs
to bursting. I serve the word
I cannot name, who names me daily,
who speaks me out by whispers and shouts.

Coming to the new year, I am picked
up like the ancient ram's horn to sound
over the congregation of people and beetles,
of pines, whales, marshhawks and asters.

Then I am dropped into the factory of words
to turn my little wheels and grind my own
edges, back on piece work again, knowing
there is no justice we don't make daily

like bread and love. Shekinah,
stooping on hawk wings prying into my heart
with your silver beak; floating down
a milkweed silk dove of sunset;

riding the filmy sheets of rain like a ghost
ship with all sails still unfurled;
bless me and use me for telling and naming
the forever collapsing shades and shapes of life,

the rainbows cast across our eyes by the moment
of sun, the shadows we trail across the grass
running, the opal valleys of the night flesh,
the moments of knowledge ripping into the brain

and aligning everything into a new pattern
as a constellation learned organizes blur
into stars, the blood kinship with all green, hairy
and scaled folk born from the ancient warm sea.

CAROL LEE SANCHEZ

~~~~~~

Corn Children

we gather our bones from many places, look for
familiar marks to determine our identities.
we share the land marks. places. buildings.
local folks.   seen with different eyes:
simon,   leslie,   paula,   and i.

i speak mostly of earth with brush and paint.
desert.   mesa.   hill and mountain.   rock.
sagebrush.   yucca and cedar.   thunders
and cloud people.

                        earth colors
                        sky colors
hand and eye proclaim on canvas and paper these
visions in my head.   in my heart.

with my brush i describe earth mother—
to remind my children the land is sacred.
this sacred alter that holds the length of one
star's breath.

with my pen i speak of relationships
with words and the ordering of them, tell little

stories.   keep hold of that harmony i am
part of.   that order of things reflected in being
                                    and spirit.

it seems proper that language should reflect harmony:
                            a giving way
                            a moving out
                            a coming in.

these things we speak about from memory
as corn children,
these traditions we keep not knowing why sometimes
or how we know the right ways.

many corn grandmothers watch over us
and whisper into the wind to remind us of our duties:

            you should never take more than you need.
            if you need some reeds for the new whisk broom
            then you go down to the river and tell the spirits
            all around you there, that you
            have come for some reeds.
            you must ask them for permission and
            then you must thank them for providing
            for you.

in this way, we keep in balance.   in this way we keep
in harmony. we should always be courteous to
everything—that's what grandma used to say.

bones of thoughts are in those burial mounds or are
around them. sometimes they are disturbed when the
mounds are plundered   but those thoughts remain
for us if we respect our ancestors.
thoughts that come to tell us:
                        that's the way it is
                        that's the way it is to be done.

spirit corn mothers watch over us.   remind us to
remember,   send their thoughts to us:

> you must respect everything that is here.
> your family, your elders, the animals.
> birds, fish,   even the rocks and bugs.
> grass, trees, sun, sky and clouds.
> you must remember these stories we tell you

we tell ourselves to remember.
     simon.   leslie.   paula.   wendy.   and i.
that we must respect everything put here   to restore
harmony.   to restore balance.

we gather our bones from many places.   examine them.
mark them.   number them.   sometimes they
speak to us.   speak through us.   become words and
pictures to pass on like the echo of grandma's words:

> you should leave one bite of food on your
> plate and offer it to the spirits.   that way
> you will always have enough to eat.
> you must remember your ancestors so they
> will remember you.

MAY SARTON

The Invocation to Kali

*. . . The Black Goddess Kali, the terrible one of many
names, "difficult of approach," whose stomach is a void
and so can never be filled, and whose womb is giving
birth forever to all things . . .*

Joseph Campbell

1

There are times when
I think only of killing
The voracious animal
Who is my perpetual shame,

The violent one
Whose raging demands
Break down peace and shelter
Like a peacock's scream.

There are times when
I think only of how to do away
With this brute power
That cannot be tamed.

I am the cage where poetry
Paces and roars. The beast
Is the god. How murder the god?
How live with the terrible god?

2
The Kingdom of Kali

Anguish is always there, lurking at night,
Wakes us like a scourge, the creeping sweat
As rage is remembered, self-inflicted blight.
What is it in us we have not mastered yet?

What Hell have we made of the subtle weaving
Of nerve with brain, that all centers tear?
We live in a dark complex of rage and grieving.
The machine grates, grates, whatever we are.

The kingdom of Kali is within us deep.
The built-in destroyer, the savage goddess,
Wakes in the dark and takes away our sleep.
She moves through the blood to poison gentleness.

She keeps us from being what we long to be;
Tenderness withers under her iron laws.
We may hold her like a lunatic, but it is she
Held down, who bloodies with her claws.

How then to set her free or come to terms
With the volcano itself, the fierce power
Erupting injuries, shrieking alarms?
Kali among her skulls must have her hour.

It is time for the invocation, to atone
For what we fear most and have not dared to face:
Kali, the destroyer, cannot be overthrown;
We must stay, open-eyed, in the terrible place.

Every creation is born out of the dark.
Every birth is bloody. Something gets torn.
Kali is there to do her sovereign work
Or else the living child will be stillborn.

She cannot be cast out (she is here for good)
Nor battled to the end. Who wins that war?
She cannot be forgotten, jailed, or killed.
Heaven must still be balanced against her.

Out of destruction she comes to wrest
The juice from the cactus, its harsh spine,
And until she, the destroyer, has been blest,
There will be no child, no flower, and no wine

3
The Concentration Camps
Have we managed to fade them out like God?
Simply eclipse the unpurged images?
Eclipse the children with a mountain of shoes?
Let the bones fester like animal bones,
False teeth, bits of hair spilled liquid eyes,
sisgusting, not to be looked at, like a blight?

Ages ago we closed our hearts to blight.
Who believes now? Who cries, "merciful God"?
We gassed God in the ovens, great piteous eyes,
Burned God in a trash heap of images,
Refused to make a compact with dead bones,
And threw away the children with their shoes—

Millions of sandals, sneakers, small worn shoes—
Thrust them aside as a disgusting blight.
Not ours, this death, to take into our bones,
Not ours a dying multilated God.
We freed our minds from gruesome images,
Pretended we had closed their open eyes

That never could be closed, dark puzzled eyes,
The ghosts of children who went without shoes
Naked toward the ovens' bestial images,
Strangling for breath, clawing the blight,
Piled up like pigs beyond the help of God....
With food in our stomachs, flesh on our bones,

We turned away from the stench of bones,
Slept with the living, drank in sexy eyes,
Hurried for shelter from a murdered God.
New factories turned out millions of shoes.

We hardly noticed the faint smell of blight,
Stuffed with new cars, ice cream, rich images.

But no grass grew on the raw images.
Corruption mushroomed from decaying bones.
Joy disappeared. The creature of the blight
Rose in the cities, dark smothered eyes.
Our children danced with rage in their shoes.
Grew up to question who had murdered God,

While we evaded their too attentive eyes,
Walked the pavane of death in our new shoes,
Sweated with anguish and remembered God.

4
The Time of Burning

For a long time, we shall have only to listen,
Not argue or defend, but listen to each other.
Let curses fall without intercession,
Let those fires burn we have tried to smother.

What we have pushed aside and tried to bury
Lives with a staggering thrust we cannot parry.

We have to reckon with Kali for better or worse,
The angry tongue that lashes us with flame
As long-held hope turns bitter and men curse,
"Burn, baby, burn" in the goddess' name.

We are asked to bear it, to take in the whole,
The long indifferent beating down of soul.

It is the time of burning, hate exposed.
We shall have to live with only Kali near.
She comes in her fury, early or late, disposed
To tantrums we have earned and must endure.

We have to listen to the harsh undertow
To reach the place where Kali can bestow.

But she must have her dreadful empire first
Until the prisons of the mind are broken free
And every suffering center at its worst
Can be appealed to her dark mystery.

She comes to purge the altars in her way,
And at her altar we shall have to pray.

It is a place of skulls, a deathly place
Where we confront our violence and feel,
Before that broken and self-ravaged face,
The murderers we are, brought here to kneel.

5

It is time for the invocation:

Kali, be with us.
Violence, destruction, receive our homage.
Help us to bring darkness into the light,
To lift out the pain, the anger,
Where it can be seen for what it is—
The balance-wheel for our vulnerable, aching love.
Put the wild hunger where it belongs,
Within the act of creation,
Crude power that forges a balance
Between hate and love.

Help us to be the always hopeful
Gardeners of the spirit
Who know that without darkness
Nothing comes to birth
As without light
Nothing flowers.

Bear the roots in mind,
You, the dark one, Kali,
Awesome power.

Birthday on the Acropolis

1

In the fifth grade
We became Greeks,
Made our own chitons,
Drank homemade mead,
And carved a small Parthenon
Out of Ivory soap.
It never seemed real,
The substance too soft,
An awkward miniature.
But over these labors
Athene towered,
Life-size.
She was real enough.

She was mine, this one,
From the beginning,
Not she of the olive,
But she of the owl-eyes,
A spear in her hand.

Any day now the air would open,
Any day ...

2

Forty years later
I was hurled to the bright rock,
Still merged with the dark,
Edgeless and melting,
The Indian ethos—
Stepped out from the plane
To stand in the Greek light
In the knife-clean air.

Too sudden, too brilliant.
Who can bear this shining?
The pitiless clarity?
Each bone felt the shock.

I was broken in two
By sheer definition:

Rock, light, air.

3

I came from the past,
From the ancient kingdoms
To this youth of my own world,
To this primary place.

I stood at the great gate
On my fiftieth birthday,
Had rounded the globe
Toward this Acropolis,
Had come round the world
Toward this one day:

O Pallas Athene,
You of the shining shield,
Give me to stand clear,
Solid as this, your rock,
Knowing no tremor.

Today, you, Pandrosos,
Who cherish the olive,
Bring from my battered trunk
The small silver leaves,
Fresh and unshielded.

Make the olives rich
In essential oil;
May the fruit fall lightly

As small drops of rain
On the parched fields.
Protect the small trees.

Today, you, Aglauros,
Pure prow of Athens,
Poise me in balance
So that all clarity
May meet all mystery
As on the spear's point.

4

When proportion triumphs,
When measure is conscious,
Who is to protect us from arrogance?

The presence of the gods. They are here:
Fate's ambiguities and jealous Athene.

No, it is not a place for youth,
This bastion where man's reason grew strong.
These pillars speak of mature power.

Imagined as white, they are rough gold,
The spaces between them open as justice
To frame mountains
And the distant, blue, world-opening sea.

5

On my fiftieth birthday I met the archaic smile.
It was the right year
To confront
The smile beyond suffering,
As intricate and suffused
As a wave's curve
Just before it breaks.

Evanescence held still;
Change stated in eternal terms.
Aloof. Absolute:
The criterion is before us.

On my fiftieth birthday
I suffered from the archaic smile.

The Return of Aphrodite

Under the wave it is altogether still,
Alive and still, as nourishing as sleep,
Down below conflict, beyond need or will,
Where love flows on and yet is there to keep,
As unconstrained as waves that lift and break
And their bright foam neither to give nor take.

Listen to the long rising curve and stress,
Murmur of ocean that brings us the goddess.

From deep she rises, poised upon her shell.
Oh guiltless Aphrodite so long absent!
The green waves part. There is no sound at all
As she advances, tranquil and transparent,
To lay on mortal flesh her sacred mantle.

The wave recedes—she is drawn back again
Into the ocean where light leaves a stain.

When a Woman Feels Alone

"When a woman feels alone, when the room
Is full of daemons," the Nootka tribe
Tells us, "The Old Woman will be there."
She has come to me over three thousand miles
And what does she have to tell me, troubled
"by phantoms in the night?" Is she really here?
What is the saving word from so deep in the past.
From as deep as the ancient root of the redwood.
From as deep as a woman's heart sprung open
Again through a hard birth or a hard death?
Here under the shock of love, I am open
To you, Primal Spirit, one with rock and wave,
One with the survivors of flood and fire,
Who have rebuilt their homes a million times,
Who have lost their children and borne them again.
The words I hear are *strength, laughter, endurance.*
Old Woman I meet you deep inside myself.
There in the rootbed of fertility,
World without end, as the legend tells it.
Under the words you are my silence.

NTOZAKE SHANGE

~~~~~~

Sechita Had Heard These Things

sechita had heard these things/she moved as if she'd
known them/the silver n high-toned laughin/
the violins n marble floors/sechita pushed the clingin
delta dust wit painted toes/the patch-work tent waz
poka-dotted/stale lights snatched at the shadows/
creole carnival waz playin natchez in ten minutes/
her splendid red garters/gin-stained n itchy on her
thigh/blk-diamond stockings darned wit yellow
threads/an ol starched taffeta can-can fell abundantly
orange/from her waist round the splinterin chair/
sechita/egyptian/goddess of creativity/2nd
millennium/threw her heavy hair in a coil over her
neck/sechita/goddess/the recordin of history/
spread crimson oil on her cheeks/waxed her
eyebrows/n unconsciously slugged the last hard
whiskey in the glass/the broken mirror she used to
decorate her face/made her forehead tilt backwards/
her cheeks appear sunken/her sassy chin only large
enuf/to keep her full lower lip/from growin into her
neck/sechita/had learned to make allowances for
the distortions/but the heavy dust of the delta/left a
tinge of grit n darkness/on every one of her dresses/
on her arms & her shoulders/sechita/waz anxious
to get back to st. louis/the dirt there didnt crawl

from the earth into yr soul/at least/in st. louis/the
grime waz store bought second-hand/here in
natchez/god seemed to be wipin hls feet in her face/
one of the wrestlers had finally won tonite/the
mulatto/raul/was sposed to hold the boomin half-
caste/searin eagle/in a bear hug/8 counts/get
thrown unawares/fall out the ring/n then do searin
eagle in for good/sechita/cd hear redneck whoops n
slappin on the back/she gathered her sparsely
sequined skirts/tugged the waist cincher from under
her greyin slips/n made her face immobile/she made
her face like nefertiti/approachin her own tomb/
she suddenly threw/her leg full-force/thru the
canvas curtain/a deceptive glass stone/sparkled/
malignant on her ankle/her calf waz tauntin in the
brazen carnie lights/the full moon/sechita/goddess/
of love/egypt/2nd millennium/performin the rites/
the conjurin of men/conjurin the spirit/in natchez/
the mississippi spewed a heavy fume of barely movin
waters/sechita's legs slashed furiously thru the
cracker nite/& gold pieces hittin the makeshift
stage/her thighs/they were aimin coins tween her
thighs/sechita/egypt/goddesss/harmony/kicked
viciously thru the nite/catchin stars tween her toes.

I Sat Up One Night

i sat up one nite walkin a boardin house
screamin/cryin/the ghost of another woman
who waz missin what i waz missin
i wanted to jump up outta my bones
& be done wit myself
leave me alone
& go on in the wind
it waz too much

I fell into a numbness
til the only tree i cd see
took me up in her branches
held me in the breeze
made me dawn dew
that chill at daybreak
the sun wrapped me up swingin rose light everywhere
the sky laid over me like a million men
i waz cold/I waz burnin up/a child
& endlessly weavin garments for the moon
wit my tears

i found god in myself
& i loved her/I loved her fiercely

Ancestral Messengers/Composition 11

they told me to travel toward the sun
to lift my feet from the soil
engage myself to the wind in a dance
called my own/
my legs, wings of lavender & mauve
they carried me to the sun-cave
the light sweet shadows eclipsing our tongues

we spoke of longings/yearnings/the unknown
we spoke in the tongue of the snake
the hoot of the owl
tongues of our ancestors
dancing with the wind

we traverse the sun
fully fired violet beings
directly overhead the sun-cave

lifting me/coaxing my eyes
to see as theirs do

crisp stalking spirits/proud
swirling spirits/my blood

they've made themselves a home here
blood relatives converging
wherever my soul is lurking
telling me   now   yes   now
go to the center of the sun

we are sending sepia stallions
headstrong appaloosas and cypress carriages
to carry you home

ALMA LUZ VILLANUEVA

Sisters

(wo)man
    Yes Woman!
I celebrate our bodies,
our wombs,
intact and perfect even as
we're born
out of our mother's
       womb
I celebrate
because most
men have forgotten
how to
he is afraid
of us, he
denies us,
   —but in the process
    denies his own existence;
    when will he re/learn
    this ancient fact—

...If man is out
of touch with
the earth,
how can he
touch woman)

I rejoice in the slick/red walls of our
    wombs,
    the milk of our breasts
    the ecstasy of our clitoris

and our need of man when we
open our legs and womb
to him
        the bloody circle thru our daughters
            and sons

I want to fly and sing
of our beauty and power.
to re/awaken this joy
in us all;
                    our power lies in being Woman

I celebrate the absence of mystery of
the 'eternal mystery of woman':
we are.

we are the trees of the earth
our roots stretching deep and strong,
the stone of the firmament,
sister to the stars
that gave birth to the soil.

Let us never forget the dance
or lose the song
or cease to dream
or efface the mystery

zero in on life
myth
magic
mystery
revel in the extra ordinary
fill your
be
ing with it,

a bird is skimming the water
lands on a smooth surface,
the snow falls softly on a mountain

chilling the earth's crust,
a sapling smiles at the wind,
a cloud gathers and spills its rain
on a hungry field,—

cock your head
and listen
it calls
    everyman
        not everyone
            hears

Creation

watching the natural slope
of my bulging stomach,   I can't
remember my bellybutton
when it wasn't turned
inside out;   and whether
I'm sitting,   standing, walking,   asleep,
    waiting for the rain,
        waiting for the sun,   a cloud,   a kiss,
            a particular shadow,
                the right noise, the correct
                    smell, the expected
                        touch
                      each separate and distinct
    moment
      I create:
      a stranger,
      sweet stranger
        floats in fleshy
          waters— we speak
            without tongues.
      cell of my cells,

                    silence and blood
                        are our translators.
and the moment of
slicing pain
        the throb and ebb of the
            sea was nothing
            compared to this)
when your minute
tears my flesh: you demand
birth—
            birth and death hot
in my thighs: I see
death grin between my legs and my
body holds back and I'm
bursting
to birth houses and trains and wheat and
        coal and stars
and daughters and trumpets and volcanoes
        and hawks and
sons and porpoises and roots and stone and
        worlds and galaxies
of humanity and life
        yet to be born: a meteor explodes!
        and you emerge
            your face a bloody
            scream between my
                thighs—traces of red/purple
                    seaweed
                    tangled and wet: you are here.
                                        you are
                                            faultless.
my precious weight
complete to itself,   attached
to the world of air:
your breathing
startles me.

Winged Woman

Winged woman, feathers
of the peacock your
stole: you stole

the rainbow — your
wings, at once,
everywhere — your

gaze before you —
your wings shaded
with light — the

sea purifies
your name
again and again —

the mountains,
proud mothers,
hold your

heart — the
snows collapse
before you, their

secrets disclose
the origin of
your birth —

the sea remembers
well your labor —
the rainbows in

the waves still
shimmer — the
stone still

waits — the whales
remember, go south;
their young swim

inside, an ocean
within an ocean.
You were always

there at the center,
beckoning me to
rise to my feet—

though I do not
see your feet,
(your gown is

long and flowing),
I know you love
the ground of

being — the air
quivers round
your massive

wings, as
wide as
you are

long. Winged
woman, my
self.

Song of the Self: The Grandmother

Surrounded by my shields, am
I:
Surrounded by my children, am
I:
Surrounded by the void, am
I:
I am the void.
I am the womb of rememberance.
I am the flowering darkness.
I am the flower, first flesh.

Utter darkness I inhabit—
There, I watch creation unfold—
There, I know we begin and end—
Only to begin, again, and again—
Again. In this darkness, I am
Turning, turning toward a birth:
My own—a newborn grandmother
Am I, suckling light. Rainbow
Serpent covers me, head to foot,
In endless circles—covers me,
That I may live forever, in this
Form or another. The skin she
Leaves behind glitters with
The question, with the answer,
With the promise:
"Do you remember yourself?"
"I am always woman."
"Flesh is flower, forever."

I enter darkness, to enter birth,
To wear the Rainbow, to hear her
Hissing loudly, clearly, in my
Inner ear: love.

I am spiralling, I am spinning,
I am singing this Grandmother's Song.
I am remembering forever, where we
Belong.

170 — Alma Luz Villanueva

Sassy

I love myself when I want
everything— when I know
everything, in my self, in
my own heart. The world does

not condone this, this kind
of knowing— the smallest child
gets whacked for such behavior.
Just this morning my three-year-
old and I fought it out at the
door— he wanted to open it,

so did I. I opened it— we both
walked through. Sometimes, I
just want to be alone in my heart,
in my soul, in my body— sometimes,

I just want to open the damn door
myself without thinking of someone
else. Sometimes, I think the best
thing we can do for our children is

to teach them how to fight
for what they want-— because
if they, too, want everything,
and dare to love themselves, they'd
better grab that handle, and when
the way is clear, pass through.

And when the way is clear, you
are alone, even if a billion
people are on your heels,
or one small child, we enter
different rooms. We could
each describe it differently—
why we came, why we stay.

Why we leave. I've been in many
rooms, and have come to realize
the fullest room was empty. To
get there you must sass back
God and fight him for the door.
And when you enter, you must
laugh at the empty fullness,
greet your perfect self in the
corner— and when she, the Goddess,
asks you what you see, as clouds,
thin air, float by: you must
answer: I see the

    freedom. She isn't pleased
or displeased—she's been expecting
you forever. She knows what
you had

to do
to love
your
self.

The Object

Embattled and twenty-two,
I went out by myself only
on Sundays. Three children
at home, not to speak

of their father, I should've
been swamped, but somehow
I made it clear—You drink,
spend money and when you

don't you're brilliant, funny,
okay, but Sundays are mine,
or at least twice a month—
because Sundays felt like

brick walls, solid steel vaults,
prison, when God was supposed
to come and make it all better,
but, damn, He only made it worse.

So, there I was, my daughter seven,
my sons five and one, and I out wandering
San Francisco trying to find a way, any
way through the walls that
I kept running into.

And, then, I saw it in a store window.
Color. Sprayed with color. A crystal
ball of color. When I held it, it felt
just right. Twenty dollars. Too much

money then. A week's groceries.
He could spend the money drinking
and I could cry, but this object
made me sweat with guilt.

Now, at forty-two, my students
say, "It's a paperweight," and,
I realize, I've never used it as one.
Instead, I've stared into it

as though it were my heart,
my womb, my brain,
and from the beginning
it's spoken to me,

giving me sympathy,
understanding, courage. This
morning I place it on my papers.
She, myself at twenty-two, would

be proud of me— the poetry,
the novel, the play, beneath—
and how I love her
for her small thefts, her stubborn

sorrow, her blazing joys that made
her settle for nothing
less than the object
of her desire.

Now, Sundays are like any other,
quieter, less cars— the one day
I must have champagne (though Mondays
are good, as well as Tuesdays, Wednesdays...)
What do I toast on these gauzy Sundays, Sunday

mornings by the sea (or close to it, anyway).
First, I toast the sun, the full moon setting
in the west, the morning star melting
into violet, the sea at low tide,
exposing her slippery womb,

the scent of life, strong and stinging
like my own. Then, the Goddess
rises up from everywhere
and I toast her and laugh—
she has no schedule.

She rises up in me, as I
hand her my paperweight—
she makes it glow
with beauty. "Settle for

nothing less," she says.
She laughs as she hands
it back to me. This Goddess
is wild, and where she laughs

things prosper, and where she
weeps things multiply in time.
She of the sun—

she of the moon—

there is only light and darkness,
and as we move between them, we
cast a shadow, and it is ours.
And as we move between them the walls

melt away, as we laugh and laugh.

                *   *   *

Settle for
Settle for nothing
Settle for nothing less
Settle for nothing less than

Settle for nothing
less than the
object of your
desire.

Desire. The weight of. The weight of our
desire. Then laugh, cry, but laugh
more than you cry, and when you hold
the world in your hands, love Her.

The Politics of Paradise

The roses blossom, scatter
in the wind—
the sun presides over beauty,
the sky is clear and lush,
the earth is ripe for love—
a man is embarrassed by his
nudity,

a woman kisses her children
goodbye,
one by one, until she is left,
finally, naked— she will
recover, fully, freely,
as the man will, as the sun
spills her pollen on him;
yellow; pale yellow, light of
fall—
the leaves spin, one by one,
freeing the tree to die—
freeing the rose to bloom—
a gathering of bees make honey,
a gathering of kisses make love—
do not sting, do not bite,
do not believe yourself un
beautiful—
the sun is out today,
the sun is out today;
yes, she is out today,
spilling pollen, her politics
of fury. Her birds of
paradise.

The world unfolds; it's
not a pebble, or a pond,
or a puzzle, but a whole
of something we call
living like the sun—
a sunbeam warms
and warns us all at
once: nurture/annihilate,
balm, burn, balm, burn—
the flowers prepare to
fly, wings outspread—
poised; orange and purple—
birds, stiff with beauty,
Earth-bound flowers.
Heal, harm, heal, harm—

the sun is like that—
but without the sun,
nothing. She who shines
for all. The politics
of paradise.

Splendid Moments

Why do I imagine that the Creator
weeps for us (I won't call her
Goddess, god, It) when our
lives tremble at their roots—

when the rain won't come—
when winter stays too long—
when love won't stay—
when soldiers do, war—

there was a time, I think,
when we knew how to plead
for rain, coax the spring,
love the bones of another,

when there were warriors
who hunted and prayed
to the wind and the animal
they longed to kill and eat.

Friends of mine have died of cancer,
bullets, no love, loss of faith,
their own hand, and as I write
of their lives, at times, I weep.

As author I spring them into being,
but then I must allow them their own
words and will if they are to live.
They teach me love.

*   *   *

And do we teach the Creator
love—does she weep for us
and laugh with us in those
spendid moments?

I would like to think so—
oh, yes— I would like to
think we are coaxing her into
being as we become.

Is this hubris—do we dare
to think she needs us—for her
becoming—that she could not
exist without us?

Does she smile at this—
does she marvel at her creation?
To dare to love is hubris,
she knows.

The Lake

(Perfect, she is, in the distance—
A woman, lying down, on
Her side, in the night. Moonlight
Lights her womb, fiercely: the lake.)

Granite ridges, sweeps of sky, sweat
upon the spine; we walk to you
carrying food, wine, warm things
to be removed, immediately; to swim

within your womb. Silky.
A pair of golden eagles scream,
spiralling, in the sky, overhead,
and I am torn between fish/fowl.

Mated pair, they greet me; they see
my spirit shining on the water;
my body is dark and hard to see.
I scream a greeting in return

and the lake stands up, womb
to womb, as the cry escapes my
throat. I am eagle. Scale
the walls, rock to rock, then up

a dry creek bed— soft moss,
delicate fern, branches whip
my arms and legs. Then,
the ledge where twin pine dreams

of the sheer drop below,
the lakes beyond, the loyal
eagles who shit on a small
sitting ledge. I edge down

to the hard, black turds,
my smelly stuff buried,
carefully, behind twin pine
dreamer. I sit, my feet dangling

off the edge, the lake below
perfect. Do you hear? Perfect.
I think of deer shit: no.
Rabbit shit: no. Chipmunk shit: no.

Then, I see the broad wings, edged
in light, spreading before my eyes;
I have climbed here to shit
with the eagles: yes.

(Snow falls, in my dreams, on
The lake, as I enter the bodies
Of strangers, a wolf, a butterfly—
Terror and wonder, alive.)

Small, fragile seed, they
crush between my fingers;
I pick one open, carefully,
a wish inside. Grant me,

I say, that I may fulfill
my dream. That is all I want.
May I complete my tasks this time.
I am your daughter. Hear me!

I let the cracked seed fall to
the ground. I enter the water.
My child holds a leopard frog.
My mate waits, patiently, following

me with his eyes until I'm gone.
I give myself to the lake, and
she receives. This is her power.
My heart is true.

(Between wake and dream
The lake sustains me,
Answers my silent questions,
At length, in depth.)

A meteor streaks down
a ridge as my eyes
open, just open,
leaving a trail

in the black night,
sliced by light, the
other stars hiss of
distance, heat, expansion,

180 — Alma Luz Villanueva

contraction, birth, the void.
Light. The infrared of meteor
and earth enter me.
There are no words for this.

No words. Lightly, I enter
this marvellous world. Lightly,
I enter ultraviolet, infrared,
como una pluma de agua.

De sueño.
De luz.
De águila.
De mi alma, silencio y cantando.

De mi alma de tierra y estrellas.
De mi alma del sol y la luna.
De mi alma de sangre y piedras.
Una pluma volando siempre jamás.

The Crux

                    1
Girl-child and amazon,
who I raised in the image
of She-who-I-couldn't-name,
but dreamt and knew when

your body slid out of mine:
daughter. Loving you, I loved
myself— badly, exquisitely.
We clung, we fought, we separated;

you to the world of men,
and I in exile. I journeyed

to the Earth and back, seeking
you in the iris, stone, the seemingly

dead bulb; and, finally, I
had to let you go, forget you,
the features of my daughter,
until my own features became

clear, distinct: separate.
Myself. Woman. And I will
die alone, and so will you.
The rose never tires of blooming.

2

She-who-I-couldn't-name
comes to me in dreams
as I walk with dark-skinned
women. She is huge and

I can't take her all in;
a belt of rainbow snakes encircles
her waist, gift of sun and storm.
Between us, daughter, lies a virgin land

where sun and moon rule,
equally; and in our loving
the land appears, vividly—
its mountains, deserts, orchards,

and the waves of natural boundaries.
Now I love myself badly, exquisitely.
Now I name the unnameable.
Now, I am your mother.

We will live and die separately,
each one virgin in her soul. The crux
of loving unsolved, but lived. The dream.
This wild rose belongs to no one.

But I offer it to you, anyway.

JULIA VINOGRAD

Motherdeath

I

Mother is dead.
Death is Mother.
Motherdeath comes to town.
Tell the world.
Tell all the worlds.
Pass it on.
Between the raised hands and the roaring drums
comes Motherdeath
with silence beneath her ribs
where no heart beats.
Her empty breasts shake
with the beaded gourds.
Between the beads of sweat on dancing skin
comes Motherdeath
with the cold she does not feel.
Between the clenched knees
and the hollow drums
go her hollow eyes.
Between the tilted throats
offered to the sun's knife
and the passed bottle
comes Motherdeath
and wine spills on bare feet.

The metal petals of a tambourine
wilt in her hands
as Motherdeath dances between the drums
> with her young face and her black hair
> full of kisses,
> with her old face and her white hair
> full of disinfectant,
> with her bone face and her own hair
> full of earth.

II

Mother is dead.
Death is Mother.
Motherdeath comes to town
Tell the world.
Tell all the worlds.
Pass it on.
At the flea market I saw her bones hidden
among antlers, goat horns, snakeskin belts,
owl wings, chicken claw roachclips,
peacock fans, alligator purses,
tortoiseshell ashtrays,
cattle skulls,
carved ivory tusks
all gathered together
by Motherdeath at night
into a patchwork beast for her to ride.
At the flea market I saw her bones scattered
between a clock without hands
and a broken cup,
between a tangle of plastic jewelry
and an Aztec calendar,
between the hot dog stand
and the free kittens mewling
with their eyes still shut,
between a yellowed wedding veil
and black leather boots,
between a noose strung with bells
and a Yugoslavian dictionary,

between a rubber machinegun
and a plate ot glass fruit,
between a 3-legged frog candle
and Prince's other glove,
between a transparent negligee
and a pair of pliers,
between a paperweight with a snow scene
and leftover christmas decorations,
between a collapsible hat
and a milk of magnesia bottle
comes Motherdeath
　　　　　with her young face and her black hair
　　　　　full of kisses,
　　　　　with her old face and her white hair
　　　　　full of disinfectant,
　　　　　with her bone face and her own hair
　　　　　full of earth.

III

Mother is dead.
Death is Mother.
Motherdeath comes to town.
Tell the world.
Tell all the worlds.
Pass it on.
Between the poised coffeehouse cigarette
and the waiting match
comes Motherdeath
painting her nails with falling ashes.
Between the smoke rings in the air
and the coffee cup rings on the table
comes Motherdeath
with her ringless fingers.
Between the pages of the morning paper
she does not look at
Motherdeath says hello
to all the other deaths
whose unmaking made the news.
"Motherdeath, I was stabbed by my lover."

"Motherdeath, a mountain fell on me."
"Motherdeath, I am one
of the estimated presumed number."
"Motherdeath, I died last night, hello."
The printed voices outline their fingerprints
upon her hands and crumble.
Between the friends that wait in line
blaming each other
for this morning's weather
comes Motherdeath
with no more weather
and she's forgotten how to wait.
Between the cups of consciousness
comes Motherdeath

> with her young face and her black hair
> full of kisses,
> with her old face and her white hair
> full of disinfectant,
> with her bone face and her own hair
> full of earth.

IV

Mother is dead.
Death is Mother.
Motherdeath comes to town.
Tell the world.
Tell all the worlds.
Pass it on.
Between the sparechangers' outstretched hands
and the shrugging crowd
comes Motherdeath:
she takes coins from her eyes
and fills their palms
with the price of everything
she cannot see,
they cannot spend,
there's only a shiver
as the lifeline twitches.
Between the slurred laughing figures

crouched around a bagged bottle
like a ring around a tub
or a ring around the moon
comes Motherdeath
scrubbing till the moon turns black
and the grimy bottle breaks.
Between the pamphleteers
and their flaring papers
(a rally, a cause,
another sale on pizza)
comes Motherdeath
who merely by listening
unsays all their words.
Between the 3 card moley dealer
and his shill
comes Motherdeath
and every card is the ace of spades,
everyone loses.
Between the vendors and their glass cases
of homemade pricetags
comes Motherdeath
with her open wallet of white worms.
Between the crazies
and their invisible monsters
comes Motherdeath
to see that the monsters
clean their plates
of every last shred of sanity
as the crazies yell and gasp
and wave their drooling fingers
and drag their melted feet behind them
not fast enough.
Between 2 guys fighting on the street
comes Motherdeath
and the swagger fades,
the swearing breaks like glass
and the dramatic spit
collected in a throat gone dry
while the cops shift

from one embarrassed foot to another
like children in church
who need to go to the bathroom.
Between the street and the street
comes Motherdeath

> with her young face and her black hair
> full of kisses,
> with her old face and her white hair
> full of disinfectant,
> with her bone face and her own hair
> full of earth.

V

Mother is dead.
Death is Mother.
Motherdeath comes to town.
Tell the world.
Tell all the worlds.
Pass it on.
Between the revolving doors of the city
comes Motherdeath
with her airless airconditioning.
Between the lunch hour businessmen
comes Motherdeath
with her briefcase full of mold.
Between the letters marked occupant
comes Motherdeath
without an occupation.
Between the crowned and cozy barstools
comes Motherdeath
and termites start chewing glass.
Between the office memos
comes Motherdeath
and the telephone weeps black tears.
Between the canned beans
and lettuce at the supermarket
comes Motherdeath
and the shopping carts bark
like poodles.

Between the junky and his vein
comes Motherdeath
and he starts to spasm;
his dope's cut
with the shadow she doesn't cast,
his vein's cut off at her source
and he's been burned.
Between the pseudo-skulls
and the adrenalin butterflies
of a rock concert
comes Motherdeath
with all her fuses blown.
Between the displays of dirty books
comes Motherdeath
and all the raincoats go limp.
Between the fire-hydrants
comes Motherdeath
and fires follow.
Between the neon urgencies
comes Motherdeath.
Between the city's loneliness
comes Motherdeath

      with her young face and her black hair
      full of kisses,
      with her old face and her white hair
      full of disinfectant,
      with her bone face and her own hair
      full of earth.

VI

Mother is dead.
Death is Mother.
Motherdeath comes to town.
Ladies and gentlemen:
make her welcome.
Pass it on.

Jerusalem

Jerusalem rises from honor as from sleep,
casting off despair, her lovely, only garment.
The prayers in Jerusalem clash one upon another
with the sound of trumpets and cymbals, and they shine.
No two prayers are alike and her prayers
are the pride of Jerusalem.
They are the hairs of her head, unbound at last and shining;
the envy of a lioness or of a languid lady.
Naked Jerusalem sings in the sun:

> "I have a lover.
> He loves me so much,
> the sun is darkened
> when we touch.
>
> I have a lover.
> He loves me so fine,
> the desert blossoms
> with restaurants and wine.
>
> I have a lover.
> He loves me so hard
> that men remember
> the art of the sword."

So Jerusalem sings, standing naked before me
with her prayers unbound about her.
She has as many sins as prayers and more,
and as many subtleties more dangerous than sin.
Look at the skeletons rotting in her mouth.
Do not look too close, she will kiss your eyes.
she will blind your eyes.
Look at her, the harlot, she is naked and unashamed.
She is singing again.
Listen:

"I have a lover.
He loves me so strong
that death turns us
into a song.

I have a lover
and a broken heart.
I cannot tell
the two apart.

I have a lover.
I have no other."

So she sings, Jerusalem, letting down her prayers for music,
and they clang together about her,
harsh and proud.
Open at last.
So:

"Color is vision
and all visions are mine.
I shall be held accountable.
Give me a flute.
O, give me a flute
and I shall charm any snake you choose
to call by my name.
I shall charm it tame as my lover is wild,
and you know who."

Reassurance

You look at me when you're bored with the world,"
Jesrusalem cried against the Lord,
"and only then, I'm a hobby for you,
a vacation for your eyes.
You wear my beauty like sunglasses
to soften the glare of things going wrong.
And they are going wrong,
I've seen black fire stir sluggishly beneath men's minds,
I've watched a compass take its clothes off,
I've heard a homesick orchid
distill poison, one inevitable drop entrapping others, like music."
She paused for breath,
shadowed with the memory of charming disasters.

"And what have you done about it?" the Lord asked her.
"Why should I do anything?"
she raised her startled eyebrow.
"If things weren't going wrong
you wouldn't wear my beauty at all.
But they are going wrong, I've seen—"
"I know," the Lord interrupted, "I've seen myself.
You're one of the things
going wrong, you know.
You might do something about it."
"*You* might do something about it," Jerusalem countered,
"I was going to lead up slowly
with classical poses and graceful reproaches and a great show
of indifferent fireworks.
You won't do anything at all then?"
"You might try yourself," the Lord suggested again.
"No," Jerusalem reassured him, "I won't take my beauty away.
You need me too much."
"I suppose I do," said the Lord without enthusiasm.

"And after all," Jerusalem added as an afterthought,
"things go wrong anyway."

Anger

Jerusalem washed her bitter hair, first in salt, then in perfumes
of cinnamon, crushed rose leaves, dark wine and one drop of blood
for decoration.
She breathed calm like armor until her aching beauty looked demure.
She took herself thus oddly equipped with cold anger to the Lord
and waited for him to notice
which happened immediately though she would have preferred
an interval of patient smiles in which to frame herself as hurt,
and make her mood both shining and expected.

"What is it?" asked the Lord.
Jerusalem laughed in her own voice,
then on a lower note,
easier, full of lush unlikely greenery and claustrophobic composure.
"I've decided to live," she informed the Lord.
"What for?" the Lord inquired, watching her closely.
"Why don't you tell me I'm already living?"
Jerusalem lost her embalmed protection
and attacked furiously,
pain singing and stabbing through her breaking voice,
"And tell me I'm already loved, while you're at it,
and that nothing else matters?"
She set her bruised archaic face like a dare against the Lord
and would not weep.
"You know all that," the Lord commented.
He watched the last of her self-control
fall like a veil full of stars
and leave her anger noble as a sword.

"What is it?" he repeated.
Jerusalem flung the sword into a fire of hungry hands
and then forgot about it.
"I thought I could live without you,"
she answered simply.
"It seemed like a good idea at the time."
"You can try," the Lord offered, "If you like."
"No!" Jerusalem wept fiercely now,

her tears many-colored as a snake's scales,
"I never said I could live without your love,
I said I could live without you.
I don't suppose it works like that."

"I see," the Lord answered gently.
"You're right, it doesn't.
It troubles me also."
"That was what I had to know," Jerusalem admitted.
"I'm sorry."
"I'm not," said the Lord.

Celebration

Jerusalem can celebrate herself
and simply ignore the two-footed armwaving believers
who explain, extoll and unroll her passion
like a piece of property.
They walk on her stone spine,
their arguments snarl in her hair,
and they all desire her skull to wear as a mask
in their rituals.
But she is alive and unmanageable,
alive and unashamed,
and worst of all
alive and unimpressed.
She'll paint a skull-mask on her face to mock them,
but always
she wears her own skin.

> And when her lovers bore her
> (she says even the Lord,
> who loves her against his will,
> but she's not always truthful);
> then Jerusalem raises her arms above her head

and throws her throat back.
Her living hair strangles all pre-packaged prayers.
Jerusalem whirls in place
becoming all directions as her bare feet gnash
and kick up sand
straight into the eyes of the Lord.

Tears of blood fall down to comfort her smile
and return to eternal confusion her worshippers
who'd thought they had her figured out at last.
Jerusalem can celebrate herself
against all ceremony,
she can wear her own skin
and show her own teeth.

DIANE WAKOSKI

The Ice Queen's Calla Lily Fingers

Little girl, whose socks were always lost
in the scuffed heels
of her shoes,
your face like a round moon showing curdy
like a blemish
in the daylight sky, the world says
you got things wrong.

Did the hibiscus of Southern California,
the humming birds like plums,
the hot air
distort your life?

You saw the Snow Queen
riding in her crystal sleigh,
not
as evil
but as refreshing goodness.
Her sky, a mirror of ice,
and its cracking splinters
NOT giving a false view of the world
but transforming
squalid or mundane reality into
an acceptable world.

Where did
the slivers of ice
stuck in my own eye
come from
in this land of orange trees
and sweet dates?

Now winter is the major season
in my life. And I contradict
the world that ice
is evil
or a signal of doom.
I know, I was not wrong,
seeing through the glassy fragment in my eye
winter's truth.
The Ice Queen
robed in ermine draws up to my door,
her crystal sleigh
invisible; her calla lily fingers
touch my door.
I go to greet her,
past tears,
wearing a cap of darkness,
the world frozen
against pain.

The Queen of Night Walks Her Thin Dog

Turning the key in the lock is the first step.
Is it an entrance or an exit
we watch?
participate in?
Singing with white hands, singing with the gloves of white hands,
singing with the grasshopper, singing with lilies of the valley, and
singing with porpoises, singing with the feet that walk over our

heads, singing with the eyes in our chins, singing for the windows
in our ankles, singing for the broken cup and singing for the
uncracked cup,

Veil.
There is a veil which will not come off.
But I sing
and it comes off. I cannot see the cup I drink out of.
But it is your cup. Cup of hot stars,
cup of crankcase oil,
cup with your beaten Egyptian lips on it. I drink through
the veil. I see through
the veil. I touch
you
through the veil. I turn the key through the veil.
I go to work through the veil. I burn through
the veil, and I sing
through the veil.

My thin racing dog
walks with me, through the night,
through the veil.
The clouds under the moon are a veil.
The circles under my eyes are a veil.
The acid in your teeth and the bone in your tongue are a veil.
The dog is a veil,
and when we sing he runs
barking
through the night. Somehow I have come
past
the veil.
The Queen of Night, running through the veil,
singing, the jewels in the foreheads of toads bursting
from my fingers. I place one
in the back

of each eye. Running through the night with my long dog
barking
passing through every house,

Passing this house,
              Entrance.
              Exit.
              The lips.

ANNE WALDMAN

Makeup on Empty Space

I am putting makeup on empty space
all patinas convening on empty space
rouge blushing on empty space
I am putting makeup on empty space
pasting eyelashes on empty space
painting the eyebrows of empty space
piling creams on empty space
painting the phenomenal world
I am hanging ornaments on empty space
gold clips, lacquer combs, plastic hairpins on empty space
I am sticking wire pins into empty space
I pour words over empty space, enthrall the empty space
packing, stuffing, jamming empty space
spinning necklaces around empty space
Fancy this, imagine this: painting the phenomenal world
bangles on wrists
pendants hung on empty space
I am putting my memory into empty space
undressing you
hanging the wrinkled clothes on a nail
hanging the green coat on a nail
dancing in the evening it ended with dancing in the evening
I am still thinking about putting makeup on empty space
I want to scare you: the hanging night, the drifting night,

the moaning night, daughter of troubled sleep I want to scare you
I bind as far as cold day goes
I bind the power of 2O husky men
I bind the seductive colorful women, all of them
I bind the massive rock
I bind the hanging night, the drifting night, the
moaning night, daughter of troubled sleep
I am binding my debts, I magnetize the phone bill
bind the root of my sharp pointed tongue
I cup my hands in water, splash water on empty space
water drunk by empty space
Look what thoughts will do   Look what words will do
from nothing to the face
from nothing to the root of the tongue
from nothing to speaking of empty space
I bind the ash tree
I bind the yew
I bind the willow
I bind uranium
I bind the uneconomical unrenewable energy of uranium
dash uranium to empty space
I bind the color red I seduce the color red to empty space
I put the sunset in empty space
I take the blue of his eyes and make an offering to empty space
renewable blue
I take the green of everything coming to life, it grows &
climbs into empty space
I put the white of the snow at the foot of empty space
I clasp the yellow of the cat's eyes sitting in the
black space I clasp them to my heart, empty space
I want the brown of this floor to rise up into empty space
Take the floor apart to find the brown,
bind it up again under spell of empty space
I want to take this old wall apart I am rich in my mind thinking
of this, I am thinking of putting makeup on empty space
Everything crumbles around empty space
the thin dry weed crumbles, the milkweed is blown into empty space
I bind the stars reflected in your eye
from nothing to these typing fingers

from nothing to the legs of the elk
from nothing to the neck of the deer
from nothing to porcelain teeth
from nothing to the fine stand of pine in the forest
I kept it going when I put the water on
when I let the water run
sleeping together in empty space
There is a better way to say empty space
Turn yourself inside out and you might disappear
you have a new definition in empty space
What I like about impermanence is the clash
of my big body with empty space
I am putting the floor back together again
I am rebuilding the wall
I am slapping mortar on bricks
I am fastening the machine together with delicate wire
There is no eternal thread, maybe there is thread of pure gold
I am starting to sing inside about the empty space
there is some new detail every time
I am taping the picture I love so well on the wall:
moonless black night beyond country plaid curtains
everything illuminated out of empty space
I hang the black linen dress on my body
the hanging night, the drifting night, the moaning night
daughter of troubled sleep
This occurs to me
I hang up a mirror to catch stars, everything occurs to me out in the
night in my skull of empty space
I go outside in starry ice
I build up the house again in memory of empty space
This occurs to me about empty space
that it is never to be mentioned again
Fancy this
imagine this
painting the phenomenal world
there's talk of dressing the body with strange adornments
to remind you of a vow to empty space
there's talk of the discourse in your mind like a silkworm
I wish to venture into a not chiseled place

I pour sand on the ground
Objects and vehicles emerge from the fog
the canyon is dangerous tonight
suddenly there are warning lights
The patrol is helpful in the manner of guiding
there is talk of slowing down
there is talk of a feminine deity
I bind her with a briar
I bind with the tooth of a tiger
I bind with my quartz crystal
I magnetize the worlds
I cover myself with jewels
I drink amrita
there is some new detail
there is a spangle on her shoe
there is a stud on her boot
the tires are studded for the difficult climb
I put my hands to my face
I am putting makeup on empty space
I wanted to scare you with the night that scared me
the drifting night, the moaning night
Someone was always intruding to make you forget empty space
you put it all on
you paint your nails
you put on scarves
all the time adorning empty space
Whatever-your-name-is I tell you "empty space"
with your fictions with dancing come around to it
with your funny way of singing come around to it
with your smiling come to it
with your enormous retinue & accumulation come around to it
with your extras come round to it
with your good fortune, with your lazy fortune come round to it
when you look most like a bird, that is the time to come around to it
when you are cheating, come to it
when you are in your anguished head
when you are not sensible
when you are insisting on the
praise from many tongues

It begins with the root of the tongue
it begins with the root of the heart
there is a spinal cord of wind
singing & moaning in empty space

How I Became Biblical

The boundary of my might wanting to be agreed upon, I travel like a note, or rather I perform as a note, a communication, a tone of definite pitch. I pitch in, sometimes out of range, a high "A," ebullient, like some wild bird cry. I listen to myself and become a woman. Then I sit down on this wide earth (Africa, Asia, South America) never to suffer again but to take on all the colors of effort it takes to be born this way. And borne along by my travelling companions, the winds, and borne along by the seed of men too, & carried the world over. I wish it for the sake of variety, complexity, science. Now see my intertidal being in all its glow & the hoopla surrounding it. I take my passport into the street to be my home metaphorically, the street which in this terroristic age could be the place of display of all freedoms & demons granted since the very beginning. I create it in my mind, too, add to it knowledge of trees, of birds, of circuity, of static, of coded messages, Molotov cocktails. My belly would be a target & my face a reflection of phenomena's desire. I would be the necessary vowels and consonants too, and condescend to speak with the breath of my 5 ancient sisters: the Winds of Thrusting, Hiding, Summoning, Gentle and Wheel. I meet them in the deserts of the world. I summon them up when you aren't looking. My scope and map are dedicated to sound reason. And my view through this lens is my passion. Let it disturb the porous, and crack the solid. It is this way I travel out of sound to be one of milk & sorrow, and one of strength & metal.

Artemis

I pray you are always above me
Imperial Ruler of The Stars
with your silver new-moon-bow,
arrows swift as science

You strike trees dead
fell a wild hind
& finally a city of unjust men
(I dreamt last night of warring Jerusalem)

Chaste sprite, spicy nymph
wounding witch, any guise you wish
No hesitation, Dakini of Incantation
Command your spike deep in my heart

so I may ride, hunt, speak, shine
mid-wife your sting.

NELLIE WONG

~~~~~~

Ode to Two Sisters in the Sun

When I eye the sun, I do not know.
Is it you two ladies sewing in your sun palace?
Is it you who prick my eyes with seventy needles,
fireworks bursting
the sky wide open?

Your silks, your embroideries overflow.
I pull your fabrics thread by thread
and still you speak no language
no dialect I understand.

You change places with your brother in the sun.
You obey the precepts
enact the virtues of modesty and shame.
The men on rooftops, in silent courtyards
expose your beauty, the power
that no one can pierce
and no one can deny.

Two sisters, will you speak out?
Will you enlighten the universe,
saturate our tongues with song?

Why did your brother go willingly
to live in the moon?
Why haven't I seen you
these long lost years?

I ride a moonboat across the sky
from beyond the sea
to the sun, your home.

Will I recognize you when we meet
and will our singing, our linking of hands
see me safely home?

ABOUT THE CONTRIBUTORS

PAULA GUNN ALLEN was born in Cubero, New Mexico, in 1939. She graduated from University of Oregon, and received her M.F.A and Ph.D. in American Studies from University of New Mexico. She has published seven books of poetry, most recently *Skin and Bones* (West End), and is the recipient of a National Endowment for the Arts fellowship. She is author of *The Sacred Hoop, Recovering the Feminine in American Indian Traditions* (Beacon) and editor of *Spider Woman's Granddaughters, Short Stories by American Indian Women* (Beacon). Professor of Native American and Ethnic Studies at University of California, Berkeley, recent National Research Council—Ford Foundation Minorities Post-Doctoral Fellow, psychic healer and mother, she is currently writing *Raven's Road*, a novel, and *The Once and Future Goddess, Female Deities and Supernaturals in Indian America*.

MAYA ANGELOU was born in St. Louis in 1928. She has published four books of poetry which have been collected in *Maya Angelou, Poems* (Random House), and recently *Now Sheba Sings the Song* (Dutton). She authored the auto-biographical series, *I Know Why the Caged Bird Sings, Gather Together in My Name, Singin' and Swingin' and Gettin' Merry like Christmas, The Heart of a Woman,* and *All God's Children Need Traveling Shoes* (Random House). She has danced, acted, directed, produced, written screenplays and musical scores for stage, motion pictures and television—notably *Georgia, Georgia*. She received the *Ladies Home Journal* Woman of the Year Award, as well as honorary degrees from Smith, Mills, Lawrence and Wake Forest Universities. She has taught dance in Europe and Israel; was a journalist in Egypt and Ghana, a teacher at University of Ghana, Northern Coordinator for the Southern Christian Leadership Conference, Commissioner for International Women's Year; and is a trustee of the American Film Institute. She is the mother of poet Guy Johnson.

JEAN SHINODA BOLEN, M.D., was born in Los Angeles in 1936, attended Pomona College and the University of California at Los Angeles and Berkeley; her major interests were the liberal arts, especially history, art history and English. She graduated from University of California, Berkeley, received her M.D. from University of California, San Francisco, was an intern at Los Angeles General Hospital, took her psychiatric residency at

UCSF—Langley Porter Psychiatric Institute, and her training in Jungian analysis at the C. G. Jung Institute in San Francisco. She is a Clinical Professor of Psychiatry at UCSF, an internationally known lecturer, and the author of *The Tao of Psychology, Goddesses in Everywoman*, and *Gods in Everyman* (all from Harper & Row). Prior to writing, she painted, and was once an art student at Los Angeles County Art Institute and San Francisco Art Institute. Poetry remains a deeply personal and private means of expression for her. She is the mother of a daughter and a son, and is one of twenty-two women in the 1986 Academy Award-winning anti-nuclear war documentary, "Women for America—for the World".

BARBARA BROOKER was born in San Francisco in 1936, and graduated from San Francisco State University. Painter, art dealer, and mother of two daughters, she published her first novel *So Long, Princess* (Morrow) in 1987, and is now completing her second novel, *Love, Sometimes*, a collection of poetry, *Contemptuous Marigolds*, and a master's degree. Particularly interested in the sociological trauma surrounding artists, she teaches workshops for women writers over forty.

JANINE CANAN was born in Los Angeles in 1942, graduated with distinction from Stanford, studied German literature at University of California, Berkeley, graduated from New York University School of Medicine, was a psychiatric resident at Herrick and Mt. Zion Hospitals, and is now a practicing psychiatrist in Berkeley. She has published five books of poetry, most recently *Her Magnificent Body, New and Selected Poems* (Manroot). She also translated the forthcoming *Psalms of Else Lasker-Schueler*. She has taught in high schools, at University of California, Berkeley, and Small Press Traffic, and has been on the staffs of Herrick Hospital and Eden Children's Center. She is currently working on a new collection of poems and essays, *Changing Woman*.

DIANE DI PRIMA was born in New York City in 1934. She attended Swarthmore for one year. She has published twenty books of poetry, including *Revolutionary Letters* (City Lights) and most recently *Wyoming Series* (Eidolon); a new edition of *Loba* as well as a selected poems are forthcoming from City Lights. She translated *Seven Love Poems from the Middle Latin* (Poets) and published an essay on H.D., *The Mysteries of Vision* (Am Here). She has received awards from National Endowment for the Arts, Committee on Poetry, and Institute for Aesthetic Development. She has taught at Esalen

Institute, Poets-in-the-Schools, Intersection, Ojai Foundation, San Francisco Zen Center, and was co-founder of the poetics programs at New College of California and Naropa Institute in Boulder, where she has taught for fifteen years. A long-time practitioner of magic, Zen and Tibetan Buddhism, Tarot, visioning techniques, homeopathy and Bach flower remedies, she now teaches at the San Francisco Institute of Magical and Healing Arts. She is currently writing *Recollections of My Life as a Woman*, a satirical novel, *Not Quite Buffalo Stew*, and a new collection of poems, *Alchemical Fragments*. She is the mother of five children, of five different fathers; and a grandmother.

ELSA GIDLOW was born in Yorkshire, England, in 1898, emigrated to Canada in her childhood, and later moved to the United States, working as a free-lance journalist, and in 1921 editing *Pearson's Magazine* in New York. She moved to San Francisco in the twenties, and later created her home Druid Heights atop Mount Tamalpais among the redwoods overlooking the Pacific, living the latter years of her life with Alan and Jano Watts, co-founders of the Society for Comparative Philosophy. She wrote poetry for seventy years, a selection of which is available in *Sapphic Songs: The Love Poetry of Elsa Gidlow* (Naiad). Some of her poems have been set to music by composers Lou Harrison and Kay Gardner. She also wrote *Ask No Man Pardon: The Philosophical Significance of Being Lesbian, Makings for Meditation, Shattering the Mirror*, and shortly before her death in 1986 completed the autobiography *Elsa, I Come With My Songs* (all published by Booklegger). She can be heard in interview on the tape "Where Eros Laughs and Weeps" (Booklegger) and seen in the film "Word Is Out.

JUDY GRAHN was born in Chicago in 1940, and graduated from San Francisco State University. She has published eight books of poetry, including *The Work of a Common Woman* (Crossing) and *The Queen of Swords* (Beacon), which will be performed by Theater Rhinoceros, San Francisco, in 1989. She has also published *Another Mother Tongue: Gay Words, Gay Worlds* (Beacon), *The Highest Apple: Sappho and the Lesbian Poetic Tradition* (Spinster's Ink) and the novel *Mundane's World* (Crossing). She has received awards from National Endowment for the Arts, American Poetry Review, Before Columbus Foundation and Women of Words. Founder of Women's Press Collective in 1970, she now teaches women's writing and mythology, and works on her ongoing project, "Women Take Back the World".

SUSAN GRIFFIN was born in Los Angeles in 1943, graduated and received her M.A. in English Literature from San Francisco State University. She has published two major collections of poetry, *Like the Iris of an Eye* (Harper & Row) and *Unremembered Country* (Copper Canyon); *Woman and Nature: The Roaring Inside Her* (Harper & Row, also published in German); *Voices*, a play (Samuel French); *Rape: The Power of Consciousness, Pornography and Silence: Culture's Revenge Against Nature*, and *Made From This Earth: An Anthology of Writings* (all from Harper & Row). She has received awards from National Endowment for the Arts, California Commonwealth Club and Women's Foundation, as well as Emmy Award, Ina Coolbrith Prize, Malvina Reynolds Cultural Achievement Award, Schumacher Fellowship and honorary doctorate from Starr King School for the Ministry. She has taught at San Francisco State University and University of California, Berkeley, publishes articles and lectures widely in Europe and America. She is currently at work on *The First and the Last: A Woman Thinks About War*, to be published by Doubleday, and *Three Plays*. She is the mother of one daughter.

JOY HARJO was born in Tulsa, Oklahoma, in 1951, attended Institute of American Indian Arts, graduated from University of New Mexico, and received her M.F.A. from University of Iowa. Her fifth book of poems is forthcoming from Wesleyan University, *In Mad Love and War*; recent books include *She Had Some Horses* (Thunder's Mouth) and *Secrets from the Center of the World* (University of Arizona). She has received awards from Pushcart, Santa Fe Festival for the Arts, National Endowment for the Arts, University of Colorado, University of New Mexico, and Academy of American Poetry. Associate Professor at the University of Arizona, and a mother as well, she is currently working on a film, "Crazy Heart/ Anna Mae Woman Warrior".

JANA HARRIS was born in in San Francisco in 1947. She has published five books of poetry, most recently *Manhattan As A Second Language* (Harper & Row). *The Sourlands* (Ontario Review) is forthcoming. She has also published the novel *Alaska* (Harper & Row) and is at work on a new one, *For The Love Of Marvel Joy*. She has taught at Modesto Junior College in California and New York University, was director of The Poetry Series at Manhattan Theatre Club, and is currently creative writing instructor at University of Washington.

ERICA HELM was born in Alturas, California, in 1954. She graduated from Grand Valley State University, Michigan, and received her M.A. in Psychology from Antioch. She has published two books of poetry, most recently *All Things Emerge* (Noh Brook), is an accomplished performance poet, storyteller and psychotherapist. She teaches workshops on "The Many Faces of the Trickster", "Creativity and Creation Myths", "Healing Stories", and "Goddesses, Saints and Heroines, Tales Empowering Women". In Washington she has received awards from King County, Vashon Allied Arts (for her "Yeats Poetry Theater") and Bumbershoot Performance Poet Competition. She is currently writing poems on Mesoamerican goddesses.

LINDA HOGAN was born in Denver, Colorado, in 1947, and is a member of the Chickasaw Nation. She graduated from University of Colorado. She has published five books of poetry, including American Book Award-winning *Seeing Through The Sun* (University of Massachusetts) and most recently *Savings* (Coffee House). She has published a book of stories, *That Horse* (Pueblo of Acoma), co-edited *The Stories We Hold Secret* (Greenfield Review), and her first novel, *Mean Spirit*, is forthcoming from Knopf. She has received awards from National Endowment for the Arts, Minnesota Arts Board and Colorado Council on the Arts. She taught American Indian Studies at University of Minnesota, now works at Birds of Prey Rehabilitation Foundation, and is a mother.

CAROLYN KIZER was born in Spokane, Washington, in 1925. She graduated from Sarah Lawrence and was a Fellow of Nationalist China in Comparative Literature at Columbia. She has published seven books of poetry, including *Mermaids in the Basement* (Copper Canyon) and Pulitzer-Prize-winning *Yin* (BOA), which contains her essay "A Muse" on her mother ("I wrote the poems for her. I still do.") A student of Roethke's, she received the Roethke Prize for *The Nearness of You* (Copper Canyon) and recently published selected translations, *Carrying Over* (Copper Canyon). She is an active reviewer, founder of *Poetry Northwest*, former Literature Specialist for U.S. State Department in Pakistan, and was first director of National Endowment for the Arts Literature Program. She has been Poet-in-Residence and Visiting Professor at various universities, has received awards from American Academy and Institute of Arts and Letters, San Francisco Arts Commission, The Governor of Washington, and honorary degrees from Whitman and St. Andrew's Colleges. She is working on *The Essential John Clare* (Ecco) and essays on Japanese fiction. She is the mother of two daughters and one son.

MARY NORBERT KORTE was born in Oakland, California, in 1934, graduated from Dominican College of San Rafael, received her M.A. in Classics from Catholic University of America, and was a member of the Dominican Order for sixteen years. She has published six books of poetry, most recently *Mammals of Delight* (Oyez). She has received awards from National Endowment for the Arts and Mendocino Festival of Books, as well as the Phelan Award, and has been California Arts Council Artist-in-Residence. She is on the board of California Poets in the Schools and is a Mendocino College English instructor. She lives in the woods at the bottom of a river canyon, and has just completed a new collection of poems, *Thunderheads & Menageries*.

MERIDEL LE SUEUR was born in Murray, Iowa, in 1900, "the beginning of the swiftest and bloodiest century". She has published five books of poetry, most recently *Rites of Ancient Ripening* (Le Sueur & Tilsen, 264 Cove Rd., Hudson, WI, 54016). She has published twelve books of prose, and her stories have been widely anthologized. Currently in print are: *Harvest and Song for My Times, 1919—1945, The Girl, Worker Writers, I Hear Men Talking*, and *Women on the Bread Lines* (West End); *Ripening* (Feminist); *North Star Country* (University of Nebraska); *Salute to Spring* (International); *Crusaders* (Minnesota Historical Society); *Little Brother of the Wilderness* and *Sparrow Hawk* (Holy Cow); and *Word Is Movement: Journal Notes from Atlanta to Tulsa to Wounded Knee* (Cardinal). "I have three books to amass," she reports, "before I leave this mortal coil." She is the great-grandmother of twenty-one.

DENISE LEVERTOV was born in Essex, England, in 1923, and moved to the United States in 1948. She has published eighteen books of poetry including *Collected Earlier Poems 1940-1960, Poems 1960-1967, Poems 1968-1972*, and most recently *Breathing the Water*, as well as two books of essays, *The Poet in the World* and *Light Up the Cave*, and a book of translations, *Guillevic/ Selected Poems*, with New Directions. She has received the National Institute of Arts and Letters, Longview, Hokins, Boulton, Zabel, Bobst, Guggenheim and Lenore Marshall Poetry awards, and honorary degrees from Colby College, University of Cincinnatti, and St. Lawrence University. She has been Poet-in-Residence and Visiting Professor at various colleges, currently teaches at Stanford, and is a foremost anti-war activist. She is the mother of one son.

LYNN LONIDIER was born in Lakeview, Oregon, in 1937, graduated from San Francisco State University and received her M.A. in Media from University of Washington. She has published five books of poetry, including *A Lesbian Estate* (Manroot), *Woman Explorer* (Painted Bride) and recently *Clitoris Lost, A Woman's Version of the Creation Myth* (Manroot). She received a California Arts Council grant to teach performance art, is a founding mother of The San Francisco Women's Building, and a "card-carrying" anarchafeminist. She currently teaches poetry to inner city children and is working on a bilingual poetry collection, *Spanish Immersion*, as well as a quartet of sexual minority novels.

AUDRE LORDE was born in New York City in 1934, graduated from Hunter College and received her M.L.S. from Columbia. She has published eight books of poetry, most recently *The Black Unicorn, Chosen Poems*, and *Our Dead Behind Us* (all published by Norton). She has also published several prose works, *The Cancer Journals* (Spinsters), *Zami: A New Spelling of My Name* (Crossing), *Sister Outsider* (Crossing), *Use of the Erotic* (Crossing), and most recently *A Burst of Light* (Firebrand). She has received awards from National Endowment for the Arts, Creative Artist Public Service, and was National Book Award nominee. She is professor of English at Hunter College and is a mother.

MARY MACKEY was born in Indianapolis in 1945, graduated from Radcliffe and received her Ph.D. in Comparative Literature from University of Michigan. Professor of English and Writer-in-Residence at California State University, Sacramento, she has published four books of poetry, most recently *The Dear Dance of Eros* (Fjord). She has also published four novels, including *The Last Warrior Queen* (Seaview/Putnam), which concerns goddess religions and matriarchy in ancient Sumeria, and more recently *The Kindness of Strangers* (Simon & Schuster). She is a translator, award-winning screen-writer, reviewer for *The San Francisco Chronicle*, and a founder of The Feminist Writers' Guild. She is currently working on a series of poems about love and destruction of the earth.

ROBIN MORGAN was born in Lake Worth, Florida, in 1941. She attended Columbia University. She has published three books of poetry: *Monster, Lady of the Beasts* and *Depth Perception* (Random House). She edited *Sisterhood Is Powerful* (Random House), *Sisterhood is Global* (Doubleday and Penguin), and co-edited *The New Women* (Fawcett). She is also the author of *The Anatomy of Freedom: Feminism, Physics and Global Politics* (Doubleday) and *Going Too Far: Personal Chronicle of a Feminist* (Random House). She received a National Endowment for the Arts grant and the Front Page Award for Distinguished Journalism. She has been professor of Feminist Studies at New College, Sarasota, Florida, contributing editor to *MS* magazine for twelve years, and a board director of the Women's Refuge, Women's Institute Freedom Press, National Alliance of Rape Crisis Centers, as well as a founder of New York Radical Women, Women Against Pornography, and the Feminist Writers Guild. She lives in New York City with her husband, poet Kenneth Pitchford, and their son Blake Ariel.

MAYUMI ODA was born near Tokyo in 1941, and graduated from Tokyo University of Fine Arts. She moved to New York in 1966. Her quest for the goddesses began when she became pregnant with her first son: "Goddesses are projections of myself, my desires, my dreams. They help me to see who I am and who I want to be." In 1981 her book of *Goddesses* (Volcano) was first published; in 1985 she was Artist-in-Residence at East-West Center, Honolulu. Her work is shown in galleries in the United States and Japan, and at the New York Museum of Modern Art, Boston Museum of Fine Arts, Cincinnati Art Museum and Library of Congress. Mayumi resides at Muir Beach, California, in a house near Green Gulch Zen Center Farm which she calls "Spirit of the Valley": "The spirit of the valley never dies./ It is called the mysterious female./ Gateway of the creating force./ It flows continuously./ Use will never drain it" (*Tao Te Ching*).

MARGE PIERCY was born in Detroit, Michigan, in 1936, graduated from University of Michigan, and received her M.A. from Northwestern University. She has published ten books of poetry, including *Circles On The Water: Selected Poems* (Knopf) and most recently *Available Light* (Knopf). She has also published nine novels, including *Woman On The Edge Of Time* and most recently *Gone To Soldiers*; a book of essays, *Parti-Colored Blocks For A Quilt* (University of Michigan); an anthology, *Early Ripening: American Women's Poetry Now*; and, with her husband Ira Wood, a play, *The Last White Class*. She was Goodridge Downs Scholar, and received the Orion Scott, Avery Hopwood, Borestone Mountain Poetry, Governor of Massachusetts Commission on the Status of Women, National Endowment for the Arts, and Rhode Island School of Design Faculty Association awards. She resides in Wellfleet, Massachusetts.

CAROL LEE SANCHEZ was born in Albuquerque in 1934, is a member of Laguna Pueblo, and the sister of Paula Gunn Allen. She graduated from San Francisco State University. She has published three books of poetry, most recently *Excerpts from a Mountain Climber's Handbook* (Taurean Horn). Also a painter, mother of three, and grandmother, she co-owns Ha-Pa-Nyi Fine Arts and serves on the boards of Santa Barbara Arts Commission, California Confederation of the Arts, California Arts Council Artists in the Schools, and Santa Barbara Urban Indian Health Clinic. She teaches workshops in the United States and Europe on Creating Urban Tribal Communities and Mother-Rite, Women-Focussed Tribal Systems; and has taught Indian and Women's Studies at San Francisco State University, San Francisco Art Institute, Mills College and California State University. A new book of her poems is forthcoming from Taurean Horn Press.

MAY SARTON was born in Wondelgem, Belgium, in 1912. She graduated from Cambridge High and Latin, and since has received twelve honorary doctorates. She has published seventeen books of poetry, including *Collected Poems, 1930—1973* (Norton), *Selected Poems of May Sarton* (Norton), and most recently *The Silence Now* (Norton). She has also published eighteen novels, most recently *The Magnificent Spinster* (Norton); a series of journals, most recently *After the Stroke* (Norton); biographies including *May Sarton: A Self Portrait* (Norton), essays and children's stories. She has received awards from University of Maine, Human Rights Campaign Fund, and the Avon/COCOA Pioneer Woman Award. She lives in York, Maine, and is completing a new novel, *The Education of Harriet Hatfield.*

NTOZAKE SHANGE was born in Trenton, New Jersey, in 1948, graduated from Barnard with honors, and received her M.A. in American Studies from University of Southern California. She has published three books of poetry, most recently *Ridin' the Moon in Texas* (St. Martin's), several plays including *for colored girls who have considered suicide/ when the rainbow is enuf* and *Three Pieces* (St. Martin's), and two novels, most recently *Betsey Brown* (St. Martin's). She has received the Outer Critics Circle, OBIE, Audelco, Silvera Writers' Workshop, and Los Angeles Times Book awards, and was a Guggenheim Fellow. She has taught at California State and Douglass Colleges. She currently lives in Houston, Texas.

ALMA LUZ VILLANUEVA was born in Lompoc, California, in 1944. At age fifteen she had her first child, followed by three more children and two grandchildren. At age forty she received her M.F.A. from Vermont College. She has published five books of poetry, including *Mother, May I?* (recently reprinted in *Contemporary Chicana Poetry*, University of California, and performed throughout Holland) and *Life Span* (Place of Herons). She has also published a novel, *The Ultraviolet Sky* (Bilingual, Arizona State University). She has received awards from University of California, University of Arizona and Hispanic Woman Making History. She teaches creative writing and is working on her second novel, *Naked Ladies*, as well as a book of poems, *Shakti*: "Sometimes it feels like swimming against the current, which we are, of course."

JULIA VINOGRAD was born in Berkeley in 1943, graduated from University of California, and received her M.F.A. from University of Iowa. She has published twenty-six books of poetry, including *Berkeley Street Cannibals* (Oyez), *Cannibal Crumbs* (Cal-Syl) and most recently *Graffiti* (Zeitgeist). She received the Before Columbus American Book Award for *The Book of Jerusalem* (Bench, out of print!) She lives in Berkeley, at work on her next book of street poems, *Horn of Empty*. For Julia the street is a symbol of the universe.

DIANE WAKOSKI was born in Whittier, California, in 1937, and graduated from University of California, Berkeley. She has published approximately fifty books of poetry, including *Trilogy* (Doubleday), *The Motorcycle Betrayal Poems* (Simon & Schuster), *Virtuoso Literature for Two and Four Hands* (Doubleday) and *Emerald Ice: Selected Poems 1962—1986* (Black Sparrow). Her *Toward A New Poetry* has been published by University of Michigan, where she has been Writer-in-Residence for thirteen years. Her poetry has been translated into Romanian, she has received awards from Guggenheim, National Endowment for the Arts, CAPS, Cassandra Foundation, Fulbright, and has taught writing at a wide variety of colleges. She is currently at work on an epic poem, *The Archeology of Movies and Books*.

ANNE WALDMAN was born in Millville, New Jersey, in 1945, and graduated from Bennington. She has published eleven books of poetry, including *Fast Speaking Woman* (City Lights) and most recently *Blue Mosque* (United Artists); *Helping the Dreamer, New and Selected Poems*, is forthcoming. She has performed her poetry throughout the United States,

Canada, Europe, and in India—in galleries, theatres, colleges, museums, festivals, films and on television—with Bob Dylan, Ken Kesey, and many other musicians and dancers; and has recorded an award-winning videotape, "Uh-Oh Plutonium". Former Director of St. Mark's Poetry Project in New York, she organized the marathon Gertrude Stein Reading in San Francisco, and is a founding director of the Naropa Institute Poetics Program in Boulder. She has edited numerous journals and anthologies, is on the board of directors of New York's Eye and Ear Theatre and the Committee of International Poetry, teaches at the Institute of American Indian Arts in Santa Fe, and University of Maine, and lectures widely. Her poems have been translated into eight languages, and she has received awards from Academy of American Poets, Poetry Societies of London and England, Poets' Foundation, Bennington College, Cultural Artists Program, National Endowment for the Arts, as well as the National Literary Anthology and Dylan Thomas Memorial Awards. She is the mother of one son.

NELLIE WONG was born in Oakland, California, in 1934, in the Year of the Dog. She studied writing at San Francisco State University. She has published two books of poetry, *Dreams in Harrison Railroad Park* (Kelsey Street) and *The Death of Long Steam Lady* (West End). She received the Women of Words Award from San Francisco Women's Foundation, and was featured in the film "Mitsuye and Nellie, Asian American Poets". She has taught at Mills College and University of Minnesota; is active in the Clericals' Union at University of California, San Francisco, where she is Administrative Assistant in the Affirmative Action Office; was organizer of the Women Writers' Union of San Francisco, a founding member of the Unbound Feet Collective, and among the first delegation of American Women Writers to travel to China. She, Mitsuye Yamada and Merle Woo will co-author a book about Asian American women in 1990 (Firebrand).

BIBLIOGRAPHY

Adler, Margot, *Drawing Down the Moon: Witches, Druids, Goddess-Worshippers, and Other Pagans in America Today*, Beacon, Boston, 1979.

Alexander, William, *The History of Women*, London, 1879.

Allen, Paula Gunn, *The Sacred Hoop: Recovering the Feminine in American Indian Traditions*, Beacon, Boston, 1986.

Andrews, Lynn, *Medicine Woman*, Harper & Row, San Francisco/New York, 1981. *Flight of the Seventh Moon: The Teaching of the Shields*, Harper & Row, San Francisco/New York, 1984. *Jaguar Woman and the Wisdom of the Butterfly Tree*, Harper & Row, San Francisco/New York, 1985. *Star Woman: We Are Made from the Stars and to the Stars We Must Return*, Warner Books, New York, 1986. *Crystal Woman*, Warner Books, New York, 1987.

Angelou, Maya, *Now Sheba Sings the Song*, Dutton, New York, 1987.

Baker, Miriam, *Woman as Divine: Tales of the Goddess*, Crescent Heart, Eugene, OR, 1982.

Begg, Ean, *The Cult of the Black Virgin*, Routledge & Kegan Paul, New York, 1985.

Benjamins, Eso, tr., *Dearest Goddess: Translations from Latvian Folk Poetry*, Current Nine, Arlington, VA, 1985.

Berger, Pamela, *The Goddess Obscured: Transformation of the Grain Protectress from Goddess to Saint*, Beacon, Boston, 1985.

Blofield, John, *Bodhisattva of Compassion: The Mystical Tradition of Kuan Yin*, Shambhala, Boston, 1978.

Bly, Robert, *Selected Poems*, Harper & Row, San Francisco/New York, 1986.

Bolen, Jean Shinoda, *Goddesses in Everywoman: A New Psychology of Women*, Harper & Row, San Francisco/New York, 1984.

Bradley, Marian Zimmer, *The Mists of Avalon*, Knopf, New York, 1983.

Brindel, June Rachuy, *Ariadne*, St. Martin's, New York, 1980.

Broughton, James, *A Long Undressing*, Jargon Society, New York, 1971.

Budapest, Z, *The Holy Book of Woman's Mysteries*, Wingbow, Berkeley, 1986.

Cady, Susan, Marian Ronan, and Hal Taussig, *Sophia: The Future of Feminist Spirituality*, Harper & Row, San Francisco/New York, 1986.

Carson, Anne, *Feminist Spirituality and the Feminine Divine: An Annotated Bibliography*, Crossing, Freedom, CA, 1986.

Chernin, Kim, *Reinventing Eve*, Times Books, New York, 1988.

Christ, Carol, ed. with Judith Plaskow, *Womanspirit Rising: A Feminist Reader in Religion*, Harper & Row, San Francisco/New York, 1979. *Laughter of Aphrodite: Reflections on a Journey to the Goddess*, Harper & Row, San Francisco/ New York, 1987.

Craighead, Meinrad, *The Mother's Songs: Images of God the Mother*, Paulist, New York, 1986.

Daly, Mary, *Gyn/Ecology: The Metaethics of Radical Feminism*, Beacon, Boston, 1978. *Pure Lust: Elemental Feminist Philosophy*, Beacon, Boston, 1984.

Di Prima, Diane, *Loba*, Wingbow, Berkeley, 1978.

Downing, Christine, *The Goddess: Mythological Representations of the Feminine*, Crossroad, New York, 1981.

Dowman, Keith, *Sky Dancer: The Secret Life and Songs of the Lady Yeshe Tsogyel*, Routledge & Kegan Paul, New York, 1984.

Eisler, Riane, *The Chalice and the Blade: Our History, Our Future*, Harper & Row, San Francisco/New York, 1987.

Engelsman, Joan Chamberlain, *The Feminine Dimension of the Divine*, Chiron, Wilmette, IL, 1987.

Fiorenza, Elisabeth Schuessler, *In Memory of Her: A Feminist Theological Reconstruction of Christianity*, Crossroad, New York, 1983.

Fortune, Dion, *The Sea Priestess*, Samuel Weiser, York Beach, ME, 1979.

French, Marilyn, *Beyond Power: On Women, Men, And Morals*, Ballantine, New York, 1985.

Friedrich, Paul, *The Meaning of Aphrodite*, University of Chicago, 1978.

Gimbutas, Marija, *The Goddesses and Gods of Old Europe: Myths and Cult Images*, University of California, 1982. *The Language of the Goddess: Unearthing the Hidden Symbols of Western Civilization*, Alfred van der Marck, New York, 1988.

Ginsberg, Allen, *Collected Poems: 1947-1980*, Harper & Row, San Francisco/New York, 1984.

Goldenberg, Naomi, *The Changing of the Gods: Feminism and the End of Traditional Religions*, Beacon, Boston, 1979.

Grahn, Judy, *The Queen of Wands*, Crossing, Freedom, CA, 1982. *The Queen of Swords*, Beacon, Boston, 1988.

Graves, Robert, *The White Goddess*, Farrar, Straus & Giroux, New York, 1948.

Grigson, Geoffrey, *The Goddess of Love*, Stein & Day, New York, 1976.

Griffin, *Woman and Nature: The Roaring Inside Her*, Harper & Row, San Francisco/New York, 1978.

Haddon, Genia Pauli, *Body Metaphors: Releasing God-Feminine in Us All*, Crossroad, New York, 1988.

Hall, Nor, *The Moon and the Virgin: Reflections on the Archetypal Feminine*, Harper & Row, San Franisco/New York, 1980.

Iglehart, Hallie, *Womanspirit: A Guide to Women's Wisdom*, Harper & Row, San Francisco/New York, 1983.

Johnson, Buffie, *Lady of the Beasts: Ancient Images of the Goddess and Her Sacred Animals*, Harper & Row, San Francisco/New York, 1989.

Kerenyi, Karl, *Goddesses of Sun and Moon*, Spring, Dallas, 1979.

Kingsley, David, *The Goddesses' Mirror*, State University of New York, 1988.

Knight, Gareth, *The Rose Cross and the Goddess*, Inner Traditions, Rochester, VT, 1985.

Le Sueur, Meridel, *Rites of Ancient Ripening*, Le Sueur & Tilsen, 264 Cove Road, Hudson, WI, 54016, 1975.

Luke, Helen, *Woman: Earth and Spirit: The Feminine in Symbol and Myth*, Cross-road, New York, 1984.

Mackey, Mary, *The Last Warrior Queen*, Berkley, New York, 1984.

Moon, Sheila, *Changing Woman and Her Sisters*, Guild for Psychological Studies, San Francisco, 1985.

Morgan, Robin, *Sisterhood Is Powerful*, Random House, New York, 1970. *Lady of the Beasts*, Random House, New York, 1976. *Sisterhood Is Global*, Doubleday, New York, 1984; Penguin, London, 1985.

Mountainwater, Shekhinah, *The Mysteries of the Goddess: A Study in the Lore and Craft of Women*, Box 2991, Santa Cruz, CA, 95063.

Noble, Vicki, *Motherpeace: A Way to the Goddess through Myth, Art, and Tarot*, Harper & Row, San Francisco/New York, 1985.

Oda, Mayumi, *Goddesses*, Volcano, San Francisco, 1988.

Olson, Carl, ed., *The Book of the Goddess: Past and Present*, Crossroad, New York, 1986.

Paris, Ginette, *Pagan Meditations: The Worlds of Aphrodite, Hestia, Artemis*, Spring, Dallas, 1986.

Parvati, Jeannine, *Hygeia: A Woman's Herbal*, Freestone, Monroe, UT, 1978.

Patai, Raphael, *The Hebrew Goddess*, Avon, New York, 1978.

Perera, Sylvia Brinton, *Descent to the Goddess: A Way of Initiation for Women*, Inner City, Toronto, 1981.

Preston, James, ed., *Mother Worship: Theme and Variations*, University of North Carolina, 1982.

Ranck, Shirley, *Cakes for the Queen of Heaven*, Unitarian Universalist, Wash. D.C., 1986.

Reed, Ellen Cannon, *The Witches' Quabala: The Goddess and the Tree*, Llewellyn, St. Paul, 1986.

Roszak, Betty and Theodore Roszak, eds., *Masculine/Feminine*, Harper & Row, San Francisco/New York, 1969.

Ruether, Rosemary Radford, *Womanguides: Readings Toward a Feminist Theology*, Beacon, Boston, 1985.

Schafer, Edward, *The Divine Woman: Dragon Ladies and Rain Maidens*, North Point, San Francisco, 1980.

Sjöö, Monica and Barbara Mor, *The Great Cosmic Mother: Rediscovering the Religion of the Earth*, Harper & Row, San Francisco/New York, 1987.

Slater, Philip, *The Glory of Hera*, Beacon, Boston, 1968.

Spretnak, Charlene, *Lost Goddesses of Early Greece: A Collection of Pre-Hellenic Myths*, Beacon, Boston, 1981. *The Politics of Women's Spirituality*, Anchor/Doubleday, New York, 1982.

Starhawk, *The Spiral Dance: A Rebirth of the Ancient Religion of the Great Goddess*, Harper & Row, San Fancisco/New York, 1979. *Dreaming the Dark: Magic, Sex and Politics*, Beacon, Boston, 1982.

Stone, Merlin, *When God Was A Woman*, Harcourt Brace Jovanovich, New York, 1976. *Ancient Mirrors of Womanhood: A Treasury of Goddess and Heroine Lore from Around the World*, Beacon, Boston, 1984.

Stein, Diane, *The Kwan Yin Book of Changes*, Llewellyn, St. Paul, 1985. *The Women's Spirituality Book*, Llewellyn, St. Paul, 1987.

Teish, Luisah, *Jambalaya: The Natural Woman's Book of Personal Charms and Practical Rituals*, Harper & Row, San Francisco/New York, 1985.

Walker, Barbara, *The Woman's Encyclopedia of Myths and Secrets*, Harper & Row, San Francisco/New York, 1983. *The Crone: Woman of Age, Wisdom, and Power*, Harper & Row, San Francisco/New York, 1985. *The I Ching of the Goddess*, Harper & Row, San Francisco/New York, 1986. *The Skeptical Feminist: Discovering the Virgin, Mother, and Crone*, Harper & Row, San Francisco/New York, 1987.

Wallis, Felicity, *Her Cycle of Transformations: A Lunar Calendar, Holladay Paganism*, 108 Montana, San Francisco, 94112, since 1979.

Warner, Marina, *Alone of All Her Sex: The Myth and Cult of the Virgin Mary*, Knopf, New York, 1976.

Washbourn, Penelope, ed., *The Seasons of Woman: Song, Poetry, Ritual, Prayer, Myth, Story*, Harper & Row, San Francisco/New York, 1979.

Weigle, Marta, *Spiders and Spinsters: Women and Mythology*, University of New Mexico, 1982.

Whitmont, Edward, *Return of the Goddess*, Crossroad, New York 1984.

Winter, Miriam, *Woman Prayer—Woman Song*, Meyer Stone, Oak Park, IL, 1987.

Wolkstein, Diane, and Samuel Kramer, *Inanna, Queen of Heaven and Earth: Her Stories and Hymns from Sumer*, Harper & Row, San Francisco/New York, 1983.

Worth, Valerie, *The Crone's Book of Words*, Llewellyn, St. Paul, 1986.

Wynne, Patrice, *The Womanspirit Sourcebook*, Harper & Row, San Francisco/New York, 1988.